C000139797

Performance

FT Prentice Hall
FINANCIAL TIMES

In an increasingly competitive world, we believe it's quality of thinking that will give you the edge – an idea that opens new doors, a technique that solves a problem, or an insight that simply makes sense of it all. The more you know, the smarter and faster you can go.

That's why we work with the best minds in business and finance to bring cutting-edge thinking and best learning practice to a global market.

Under a range of leading imprints, including *Financial Times Prentice Hall*, we create world-class print publications and electronic products bringing our readers knowledge, skills and understanding which can be applied whether studying or at work.

To find out more about Pearson Education publications, or tell us about the books you'd like to find, you can visit us at **www.pearsoned.co.uk**

PEARSON
Education

Performance

The secrets of successful behaviour

Robin Stuart-Kotze

FT Prentice Hall
FINANCIAL TIMES

An imprint of **Pearson Education**

London • New York • Toronto • Sydney • Tokyo • Singapore • Hong Kong
Cape Town • New Delhi • Madrid • Paris • Amsterdam • Munich • Milan

PEARSON EDUCATION LIMITED

Edinburgh Gate
Harlow CM20 2JE
Tel: +44 (0)1279 623623
Fax: +44 (0)1279 431059
Website: www.pearsoned.co.uk

First published in Great Britain in 2006

The right of Robin Stuart-Kotze to be identified as author of this work has been asserted
by him in accordance with the Copyright, Designs and Patents Act 1988.

ISBN-13: 978-0-273-70798-1
ISBN-10: 0-273-70798-1

British Library Cataloguing in Publication Data
A catalogue record for this book is available from the British Library

Library of Congress Cataloging in Publication Data
A catalog record for this book is available from the Library of Congress

10 9 8 7 6 5 4 3 2 1
10 09 08 07 06

Designed by Sue Lamble
Typeset in 9.5pt Stone Serif by 70
Printed in Great Britain by Henry Ling Ltd., at the Dorset Press, Dorchester, Dorset

The Publisher's policy is to use paper manufactured from sustainable forests.

*To wonderful Lorna for her unflagging support and
encouragement and for her many brilliant ideas, all of which I am now
pretending are mine.*

Contents

Preface

Those who write clearly have readers; those who write obscurely have commentators. (Albert Camus)

The eternal question in organizations is 'How do you improve performance?' This book provides the answer to that question.

Behaviour is what drives performance. Personality is not the issue. Definitive research shows that less than 10 percent of the variance in a person's behaviour is explained by personality. This book is about behaviour and how to channel it to create top-level performance.

In his book *The Wisdom of Crowds* James Surowiecki makes the point that if you ask a big enough and diverse enough group of people to give their answers to a problem, their conclusion will be superior to that of any individual, no matter how smart the individual is. And that's how we learned the secret of how to improve people's performance: we talked with more than 5,000 managers over a period of three decades. And, more importantly, *we listened to what they said*.

Surowiecki says there are four conditions that make a group of people smart: diversity of opinion, independence (meaning their opinions are not influenced by other people in the group), decentralization (meaning the people come from different backgrounds and different situations), and aggregation (meaning that there is a way of bringing all their opinions and decisions together to form the consensual picture). Our 5,000 people came from North America, Europe, Asia, Africa and

Australia; they came from a myriad of different companies – commercial and non-profit, professional and industrial, service and manufacturing; they had different views and different opinions and they weren't at all shy about expressing them; and we wrote down all the things they told us and watched the consensus picture form.

This book is about a science of successful behaviour. Unfortunately the word 'science' is intimidating to some individuals. It conjures up images of people in white coats with blackboards covered in arcane mathematical formulae and equations. But it's simply, as *The Oxford Dictionary* says, 'the systematic study of the structure and behaviour of the physical and natural world'. Nothing too frightening about that. So there you have it: all we've done is systematically study the phenomenon of behaviour in organizations and analyzed how it either improves, sustains or blocks performance. It wasn't overly difficult; it just took a long time. But we think you'll agree that the results were worth it.

There is no clearly defined field of endeavour that focuses purely on behaviour change and performance improvement in an organizational context. Books, articles, cases and research studies draw upon theories and findings across the entire range of the social sciences – economics, psychology, sociology and anthropology – with little or no integrating thread. The so-called field of organizational behaviour is an amalgam of all these disciplines. However, extensive experience and research of change, and many long conversations with people doing it successfully and unsuccessfully has led to a distillation of the underlying basic principles of performance improvement. We have called it *Behaviour Kinetics* – the science of behaviour change.

But don't let the fancy terminology deter you. Behaviour Kinetics is simply a set of facts that underlie successful behaviour change. They are not complex and you don't have to have a white coat or deal in higher mathematics to understand them. They are:

- Personality does not determine performance.

- Behaviour determines performance.

- There is no ideal set of behaviours that consistently leads to high-level performance.

- The thing that determines whether any specific behaviour is successful is the job itself.

- The person who knows how to do a job best is the person doing it.

- To improve your performance you need to understand precisely what you are doing now.

- Once you know what you are doing currently, you need to know what you should be doing differently if you want to improve your performance.

- Without clear measurement, change becomes random.

- People change because they want to, not because someone else wants them to.

- Asking people what they should do to improve performance is far more effective than telling them. As Winston Churchill so nicely put it, 'Personally I'm always ready to learn, although I don't always like being taught'.

Einstein's dictum was that 'Everything should be made as simple as possible, but not simpler'. Behaviour Kinetics is not psychobabble; it doesn't require any special knowledge or qualifications to understand or implement; it doesn't involve long lists of things or complicated models; it applies to anyone in any job, in any industry or profession, in any country. It produces guaranteed results. Its shining example is the culture and processes of Toyota, the world's most successful car manufacturer.

The book

There are summaries at the end of each chapter, so we won't bore you by repeating them here. If you want to skim the book, the summaries are a good place to start. This is not a dry academic tome. It's written in everyday language, hopefully in an entertaining way, and it tries to tell it like it is. Telling it like it is, of course, is a euphemism for being opinionated. In one of her famous songs in the roaring twenties Sophie Tucker maintained that 'Fifty million Frenchmen can't be wrong'. The opinions in this book are a reflection of only a small percentage of that number of people, and an even smaller percentage of them are French, but we're happy to use Sophie's line as the precedent. However, we can't just sit behind that defence and shrug off argument on the basis that we're only reflecting what others have said. This book isn't just about business; it's also personal. If you agree with it, thank the 5,000; if you don't, there's only one name on the front cover and I'll tell you where to find me.

The book is in two parts. The first part presents the ideas and processes of the science of successful performance. Part 2 of the book presents four case studies that demonstrate a data-based approach to performance improvement. In each case, the behavioural data used to effect change has been gathered with the use of a diagnostic tool. Slowly – some would say far too slowly – organizations are realizing the importance of gathering hard data on which to base their decisions about people. All the major functional areas of organizations – marketing, finance, accounting, manufacturing, assembly, quality control, supply chain, logistics, etc. – generate as much hard data as they can, and they use this data, rather than unquantifiable models, to make decisions. The one area where data-based decision making lags behind is the management of people – leveraging their skills and knowledge, motivating them, enabling them constantly to improve their performance. It's time to correct that. Hopefully this book will stimulate much more work in this area. You can't have a science of behaviour change without applying some scientific tools.

A book of this kind is never the work of a single person. Heartfelt thanks are owed to a number of people who read early drafts and who made helpful comments and suggestions: Robert Cochrane, Alan Yu, David West, Gavin Kotze, Corinne Hay, Mono Jethwa, Tony Scanlan, George Campbell, Mark Reynolds, Chris Tomkinson, Kevin Howes, Tom Mellin, Janet Chamdal, Peter Nixon and Scott Lyall. Thank you very much.

The conversations leading up to the book took place over three decades and the book went through three writings. Each time it got better. Special thanks to Richard Stagg at Pearson for jolting it into final focus.

If one wanted to find a perfect example of excellent performance, the team at Pearson who have managed this book is it. My deepest and most sincere thanks to Liz Gooster, Elie Ball, Lucy Blackmore and Laura Brundell for everything they have done to make this book work. They are paragons of professionality – and also lots of fun. I'm looking forward to the next book already.

The wonderful dialogue with the 5,000 individuals also just got better and better as we went through the years, and now is not the time to end it. The great Peter Drucker, who *Business Week* called the 'man who invented management', said 'The only true expert is the person who does the job'. If only more people listened to them. My email is kinetics@behaviouralscience.com. I look forward to a conversation with you.

Robin Stuart-Kotze

part
1

The science of successful behaviour

1

Performance:
it's about behaviour

I'm no better or less than the next man. But the thing about me is that
I always knew what my acts would mean. (Vince Lombardi)

Do you know how you get results in your job? Are you clear on what
makes a difference and what doesn't? Do you know how you drive
performance? You do hundreds of different things each day, but the
results you achieve are driven by a handful of them. The rest don't really
have much of an effect; they just absorb energy, emotion and time. So
what do you need to do to really make a difference? This book gives you
the answer to that question.

Behaviour drives performance

The thing that drives performance is behaviour – how you act. It's what
you *do* that matters, not what you are or who you are. *The Oxford
Dictionary* defines behaviour as the way in which one acts or conducts
oneself. Behaviours are the actions you take and the decisions you
make. You can control these things: you can decide what to do and
when to do it. And because you can decide what to do in any situation
you can determine your performance. High-level performance results
from doing the right thing at the right time. In tennis, excellent performance doesn't result from simply hitting the ball over the net into the

other court; it's hitting it to the right place in the other court, and at the right speed. In golf it's not just a matter of hitting the ball straight (although most golfers would kill to be able to do that consistently); it's hitting the ball the right distance with the right loft and with the right amount of spin.

Performance is all about doing the right thing at the appropriate time. The big questions, of course, are 'What's the right thing to do?' and 'When's the right time to do it?' The answers are different for every job, and while that sounds as though it makes things exceedingly complex, there are processes that, if followed, make it all quite manageable. This book outlines those processes.

What is the difference between behaviour and personality?

Our focus in this book is purely on behaviour. It's what you *do* (behaviour) that determines your performance, not what you *are* (personality). It is absolutely critical not to confuse behaviour with personality. To repeat: personality is what you are; behaviour is what you do, and it's what you do that makes a difference. When Stuart Pearce, the manager of Manchester City football club and a former captain of England, was asked what drives performance, his immediate response was 'behaviour'. When asked whether the personalities of his players made a difference, his view was that while their personalities

❝ no matter what the personality, results come from behaviour ❞

meant they needed to be motivated differently, what they actually did on the field was what made a difference. The answer is clear: no matter what the personality, results come from behaviour.

However, most people believe that personality determines how individuals act, and it's very difficult to shake that belief. Personality testing is widely used in recruiting, with the underlying assumption that it will predict how people will behave in a job, and therefore will determine their performance. But if personality were the key to performance, then how can you explain the success of three people with very different personalities? Everybody's heard of Richard Branson, probably because of his flamboyance and seemingly extrovert personality. But you've probably not heard of A.G. Lafley or Darwin Smith. Both of them have performance records that are absolutely outstanding. Lafley is the CEO of Procter & Gamble. Since he took charge of P&G in 2000 he's grown the company's volume, exclusive of acquisitions, by 10 percent a year, and more than doubled the stock price. If you count major acquisitions, the most recent of which has been Gillette, the growth figures are astronomical. *Fortune* magazine called Lafley 'The un-CEO' because of his quiet and undemonstrative personality. He's the polar opposite to Richard Branson. Darwin Smith was CEO of Kimberly-Clark for 20 years and during that time the company had cumulative returns four times that of the stock market as a whole. Over his 20 years as CEO Smith turned Kimberley-Clark from a fading paper company whose stock lagged the market by 36 percent to the leading paper-based consumer products company in the world. Now *that's* performance. But Darwin Smith is described as having an 'awkward shyness and lack of pretence' and as a man who had no airs of self-importance. Yet Branson, Lafley and Smith are all absolute top-level performers. Clearly, it isn't personality that determines performance.

A critical difference between behaviour and personality is that your personality is essentially fixed at an early age and after that you can't really change it. Given that we live in an age of continuous and rapid change, unless the job you are in remains completely static you're in trouble. Until quite recently it has been accepted that personality is basically established somewhere around the age of five. The precise age has been the subject of discussion. However, a major study published by Caspi et al. in 2003 showed that the personalities of a thousand children (a sample size that makes the conclusions of the study fairly robust) tested at age three and then re-tested 20 years later *had not changed*. You are what you are by the age of three and it doesn't change after that. The Chinese have known this for centuries. There is an old Chinese saying: 'Age three determines age eighty'. Perhaps if the researchers had known this they could have been saved 20 years of work.

But although you are what you are and you can't change your personality, you *can* change what you *do*. The major determinant of performance is behaviour. Personality gets the headlines because people would like to find a secret key to success that does not require work and effort. Stephen Covey, in his best-selling *The Seven Habits of Highly Effective People*, remarks that 'The glitter of the Personality Ethic, the massive appeal, is that there is some quick and easy way to achieve quality of life . . . without going through the natural process of work and growth that makes it possible'. The reason that the idea of classifying people by personality types is so attractive is because it means that instead of having to deal with an almost infinite array of differences we only have to deal with a small number. The assumption is that if you fall into a particular personality type you will behave just like everyone else who is that type. It's really not that different from astrology. And as far as predicting or determining performance is concerned, it's about as effective.

Personality is a poor predictor of performance

Personality is simply another word for characteristics. People's person-alities can be described, in everyday language, by words like friendly, open, adaptable, pessimistic, creative, dominating, flexible, inquisitive, shy, optimistic, conscientious, outgoing, etc. These characteristics describe the general demeanour of an individual – how he or she tends to be perceived by others (at least some of the time). But general charac-teristics don't predict behaviour very well. We do different things when we are faced with different situations, regardless of what our basic personality may be.

You probably find it difficult to accept that personality is a poor predictor of performance – in spite of the example of the highly different personalities of Richard Branson, Darwin Smith and A.G. Lafley, which had no discernable effect on their ability to lead and manage at the highest level of competence. One of the reasons we find it hard to accept personality is a poor predictor of performance is that we are constantly bombarded with all kinds of information to the contrary. About four million people a year complete the Myers-Briggs Type Indicator, one of the most widely used personality tests in the world. They must think it's worth their while to do it. And lots of influential people in companies must think it's useful because 89 of the Fortune 100 companies use it. There's an excellent chance you've completed a Myers-Briggs or some other personality inventory at some stage in your career.

The proponents of personality tests claim that they make people more sensitive to how they behave, and how other people behave and the result is therefore greater work effectiveness. However, in their book *In the Mind's Eye: Enhancing human performance*, Daniel Druckman and Robert Bjork, two eminent psychologists, comment that 'Unfortunately, neither the gains in sensitivity nor the impact of those gains on performance have been documented by research'. Annie Murphy Paul, author of *The Cult of Personality*, is equally blunt: 'There is scant evidence that [personality test] results are useful in determining managerial effectiveness, helping to build teams, providing career counselling, or enhancing insight into self or other'.

The definitive research into the relationship between personality and behaviour was conducted by Stanford professor Walter Mischel. Studying the correlation between personality tests and people's actual behaviour, he found that less than 10 percent of the variance in a person's behaviour is explained by personality. The driver of people's behaviour, he observed, is in fact the situations in which they find themselves – and most importantly, that their behaviour changes as the situation changes.

This is the heart of the issue. Nobody likes to fail, so we do what we think will make us succeed. You change your behaviour depending on the situation with which you are faced. But in spite of the fact that we know this to be true, we would prefer to believe, as Stephen Covey observes, 'that there is some quick and easy way to achieve quality of life . . . without going through the natural process of work and growth that makes it possible'. We want to believe that there is a simple way of categorizing people. Descriptions of personality types are excellent subjects for what psychologists term 'projection': that is, projecting one's feelings, beliefs, attitudes, etc. onto something. The classic experiment that proved that this is exactly what happens was conducted by Bertram Forer. He gave a group of individuals a personality test and then handed them back their results – ostensibly the results from the test, but in fact randomized astrological forecasts from a book he had bought at a nearby news-stand. When he asked the individuals how accurate they found their profiles, on a scale of 0 (poor) to 5 (perfect), 40 percent gave a perfect 5 and the average score for the group was 4.2.

Personality is a very poor predictor of performance because people are actually highly adaptable and far more flexible than personality typing gives them credit for. Personality tests cannot and do not predict how people will act in a variety of roles or situations. Nor are they able to predict how behaviour changes over time. These are the immutable facts on which everything in this book is based. If you're still undecided about accepting these facts, then read on and see them demonstrated in practice. If you simply cannot accept them, then now is the time to put the book down.

How you behave in your job is a matter of the requirements of the job. Take a minute here and think of two jobs you've had that were very different from one another. In each case write down the three things you did that made the greatest impact on your performance in the job. Were they the same three things in each case? If the jobs you were thinking about were really different from one another, then it's unlikely.

We do things that, given the situation, work for us, and to do that we unconsciously assess the situation and make a judgement. When we do that we're using a part of the brain that is known as the adaptive uncon-scious. Like it or not, you adapt your behaviour to different situations. People who don't adapt their behaviour to the situation stand out as misfits. Ricky Gervais' character in the television series *The Office* is a good example of the inability to understand situational differences and their differing behavioural requirements.

Before we appear to wash away the concept of personality completely, it must be said that understanding your personality is useful in that it gives you a sense of the range of behaviour with which you may be most comfortable. Your underlying personality describes how you would prefer to behave if, to use the economists' phrase, 'all things were equal' – i.e. if there were no situational requirements for specific behaviours other than the ones in which you would most like to engage. For instance, some people prefer to work with structure and detail while others don't handle detail well and bridle at having to conform to systems and procedures. However, that does not mean that either of these types of people can't do the things they don't prefer to do. Personality typing often gives people an excuse not to adapt their behaviour to changing situations. 'I'm not good at detail. It says so in my personality profile. So you just have to understand that I can't deal with a job that requires attention to detail.' Rubbish. If that individual were trapped in a burning building and it was necessary to perform some detailed operation to get out, they would be able to focus on the minutest of detail.

If you consistently avoid doing things that you don't particularly like, you are likely to become worse and worse at them. On the other hand, when you enjoy doing something, you tend to do more of it. That's called practice, and practice improves performance. Since in most cases performance is what allows you to keep your job, or to advance in your job, it's not a bad idea to practise some of the things you aren't really fond of doing, because they have a nasty habit of being required from time to time.

> **" personality typing often gives people an excuse not to adapt their behaviour "**

If it's not your personality, what determines your behaviour?

The effectiveness of any action depends on the situation. To repeat, effective performance in a job results from doing the right things at the right time – the right things for that specific job at that specific point in time. Easy to say, but not always quite so easy to do. What makes it difficult, of course, is determining what these 'right things' are. Despite what hundreds of management books would have you believe, there isn't a simple list of behaviours that top-level performers exhibit – i.e. a prescription of behaviour that will unfailingly lead you to success. Take a look at the behaviour of five or six top-level performers in different occupations, jobs or professions and you'll find that they do a lot of things differently from one another. Just read the biographies of five or six business leaders, military leaders and political leaders. They're all different. There isn't a universal list of 'must dos' that unfailingly result in high performance.

Extensive research into traits of effective leaders has failed to find any correlation between one particular set of traits and success. This is not a matter for debate. It is hard, scientifically proven fact. Any individual, any article or any book that purports to tell you that there is a set of behaviours which, if you exhibit them, will unfailingly result in success is either living in dreamland or engaging in fraud. The reason, of course, is that situations vary.

The problem with trying to identify a list of behaviours that always have a positive effect on performance is that there are hundreds of factors that make every job and every situation different. For instance, delegating responsibility to people is a behaviour that is almost universally said to lead to improved performance. But what if the people to whom the responsibility for performing a task is delegated don't have the necessary skills, knowledge or resources to do it? That's asking the incapable to do the impossible, and its results are predictably disastrous.

What determines whether any behaviour is effective or not is the situation in which it is applied. Give detailed instructions of how to get somewhere to a person who has never made the journey and doesn't know which route to take and you'll probably be thanked. Do the same thing to someone who knows the route backwards and travels it frequently and at best you'll annoy them, or at worst offend them.

To perform any job or role well means that certain specific things must be done. Jobs all have what might be termed 'behavioural demands' – i.e. specific behaviours that are necessary to manage the job effectively. Every job has its own set of particular behavioural demands. For instance one job may require detailed attention to planning, another may require that all involved parties contribute to decisions, and still another may require that a single individual sets a clear example of behaviour that people will follow and emulate. These are very different collections of behaviours. If a job requires its incumbent to involve people in decisions and that individual is continually mired in creating detailed plans that don't involve others, things are not going to go well.

Therefore, to perform a role effectively you need to have a clear picture of the behaviour required by the role in order that you can do the right things – i.e. the things that lead to performance improvement – and not the wrong things.

The effectiveness with which an individual manages their job – i.e. the level of performance that is achieved – is dependent on the degree to which their behaviour matches the behavioural demands of the job. Figure 1.1 illustrates this. The greater the overlap of the two circles, the higher the level of performance.

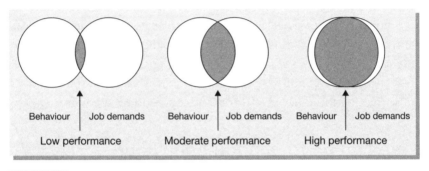

Figure 1.1 Levels of performance

Performance and adaptability

The *Harvard Business Review* (January 2005) ran an article by Dan Ciampa entitled 'Almost ready: how leaders move up'. It wasn't about just any move up the organizational ladder; it was about the move to CEO. But even though the article focused on this one particular career move, the point it made was that jobs can be very different from one another and the behaviour that makes an individual successful in one job won't necessarily be what makes them successful in another. The ability to adapt your behaviour to changed circumstances lies at the heart of effective performance.

We followed the careers and behaviour of a hundred or so managers in a Canadian utility company for a period of seven years and asked them to complete a behaviour questionnaire at the end of every year and/or each time they changed jobs. Those managers who changed their behaviour to meet the changing demands of their jobs maintained an upwardly mobile career pattern. Those who maintained relatively unchanged behaviour over a period of time either remained stagnant in their jobs or left the company.

Failure to change continually is terminal. As the great Edwards Deming, the father of the quality movement, put it, 'It is not necessary to change. Survival is not mandatory.' The game is constantly being raised. The competition gets tougher and tougher. You have to be better at your job than your predecessor – and if you want to avoid paving the way for a premature successor with your pink slip, you need to become better still.

Performance improvement is about examining your current behaviour, recognizing what you need to do differently, entertaining new ideas, and consciously changing your behaviour to meet the changing requirements of your job. It's what every successful person in business does. It's what every top-class professional athlete does. They know that failure to raise their performance means that the competition will beat them.

The motivation to change behaviour

Decisions to change behaviour are based on one of two things: an image of potential or a feeling of pain. The folksy way of saying this is that people change what they're doing either when they see the light or when they feel the heat.

People never change their behaviour without either being attracted to the light or repelled by the heat. If you're comfortable, what's the point of behaving differently? The saying is 'If it ain't broke, don't fix it'. The only problem is that there is a continuum between 'running in perfect order' and 'broke', where things are slowly breaking down but aren't noticeable. The bearing is slowly being worn down, the lubricant is slowly disappearing, but the mechanism is still working just fine – until the bearing seizes. The fact of the matter is that your job, whatever it is, is changing continually. The objectives are moving, the processes are changing, the technology is improving, customers' expectations are changing, and competition is stiffening. But all these things are creeping up quietly and slowly, just below the radar, until all of a sudden they appear, flashing madly on the screen, and then it's all hands to battle stations.

Some behaviour changes may be due to sheer chance, but generally they follow what the psychologist Edward Thorndike called the law of effect. It states that behaviours followed by reward are strengthened, and behaviours followed by punishment are weakened. In other words, behaviour is modified by its consequences. If you can, you do things that have positive consequences, and you stop doing things that have negative consequences.

❝ your job, whatever it is, is changing continually ❞

Homer's epic poem, *The Odyssey*, begins each verse with the beautiful line, 'Dawn comes early, with rosy fingers'. An organizational version of *The Odyssey* might begin each of its verses with the line, 'Change comes furiously, with slashing claws'. Sometimes change is like an earthquake. All of a sudden there's a merger, a takeover, a downsizing, a new process, a new corporate vision, new objectives, a new competitive threat, a rapid shift in consumer tastes, a new technology, a killer application. The game hasn't just changed from softball to hardball; it's become a completely different game with different rules.

However, in most instances the verse should begin, 'Change creeps silently, with softly twining tentacles'. Change is generally incremental. It only appears as sudden and violent because we've failed to notice the tiny movements of a never-ending series of small things, until all of a sudden they have massed themselves into a huge wall that threatens to come tumbling down on us. In our day-to-day work we are faced with a constantly changing situation. If you look at Figure 1.2 you begin to see

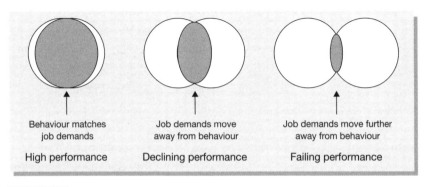

| Behaviour matches job demands | Job demands move away from behaviour | Job demands move further away from behaviour |
| High performance | Declining performance | Failing performance |

Figure 1.2   Changing behavioural demands

what happens when the behavioural demands of the job continue to change and the things you do to manage the job (your behaviour) don't.

Think about the job you're doing now and what your job was 12 months ago. Think about what's remained the same and what's changed. The list of things that have changed – the different things you now have to do to perform your job well – will surprise you. If you think that you're on top of your job right now and you couldn't do it any better, you've probably just fallen behind.

Everyone knows the parable of the frog. If one is sadistic enough to put a frog in a pot of warm water and then slowly heat the water, the frog will not detect the incremental temperature change and will boil to death. The implication is that we're just like frogs. But we don't have to be. While the frog may not have processes at its command that allow it to monitor the very slow temperature change, we do. We have available to us both heat sensors and light meters. If we want to take regular readings we can see when the heat is rising and when the light is becoming brighter. We just have to take the readings continuously and then act accordingly. An analogy is weight control. If you want to control your weight, weigh yourself every day. If you gain a pound, it's easy to deal with. If you gain 20, it's hard work.

Continuous performance improvement

Behaviour change is all about performance improvement. No one changes what they're doing so that they can worsen their performance. Golfers don't get on the practice tee to try to accentuate their slice. Sales people don't try to make a practice of things that lose them sales. Banks don't make loans they are certain will never be repaid. But there's a very big difference between what might be called big-bang performance improvement – major change programmes, sweeping productivity initiatives, across-the-board restructuring, etc. – and continuous performance improvement. The former is traumatic, difficult and has a high casualty rate. The latter avoids any bang. It isn't traumatic and it doesn't leave blood on the floor. It doesn't require pulling out the 'escape from the jaws of death' battle plan, because it puts people and organizations out in front of the turbulence.

This book is about creating continuous performance improvement – both personally and within your organization. It's not about a 'great leap forward'. Mao Zedong tried that and it didn't work. It's about creating a momentum for continuous, incremental improvement that moves you and/or your organization steadily up through the field, establishing a lead *and staying there!* We've all been subjected, willingly or unwillingly, to various one-shot initiatives that bump up performance in the immediate to short term. But they're a bit like fad diets: you lose some weight quickly and then put it back on almost as quickly. The difference with continuous performance improvement is that rather than producing a graph that shows a sharp rise and then a decline, it shows a graph that not only moves upward but does so at an ever-increasing pace.

Continuous performance improvement (CPI) is focused on what *you* can do and what *you* can change. It is about things that are within your control. You make the difference. It's not theory; it's a scientific approach that's based on behavioural fact. It involves accurate measurement, not sketchy approximation. It's based on hard data, not subjective opinion. It's a proven process that has worked in all types of organizations.

Chapter summary

Performance matters. Everybody and everything is measured by performance. Do you know how you get results in your job? Of the myriad things you do every day, what gets results and what doesn't? Behaviour drives performance: it's what you do that makes a difference. High-level performance results from doing the right things at the right time.

Personality is a poor predictor of performance. Definitive research by Walter Mischel of Stanford found that personality predicted less than 10 percent of behaviour. If we accept that behaviour drives performance, then personality is not the key. Performance is determined by what you do (behaviour), not what you are (personality). The thing that determines behaviour is the situation. How you behave in your job is a matter of the requirements of the job. Your effectiveness is therefore a matter of matching your behaviour with the requirements of the job.

The ability to adapt your behaviour to changing circumstances lies at the heart of effective performance. Performance improvement is about assessing the demands of the situation, examining your current behaviour to determine its appropriateness or fit, and adjusting what you do to meet the challenges.

People change their behaviour either when they see the light or feel the heat. Change is continuous but incremental; things change imperceptibly but incessantly. As the demands of jobs change – technology, competition, objectives, resources, responsibilities, skills, knowledge, etc. – behaviour must change to meet these demands.

2

Changing behaviour

Only those who adopt change survive. (Charles Darwin)

You can't manage what you can't measure. You can't measure what you can't describe. (Robert Kaplan and David Norton)

An old Harvard professor, Fritz Roethlisberger, used to say, 'It's not what you don't know that hurts you, it's what you know that isn't so.' A lot of the so-called accepted wisdom about change is rubbish: it's value-laden, prescriptive and unsubstantiated in practice. There is a strong whiff of nannyism and holier-than-thouism about much of it. If you plan to read about the subject, be prepared to kiss a lot of frogs before you find a prince.

However, if you want to start off with a prince, try reading John Kotter's books (see References). They are based on extensive, rigorous research, and deal with the real world. Kotter's research into the core problems that all change initiatives face has led him to conclude that 'The central issue is never strategy, structure, culture, or systems. All those elements, and others, are important. *But the core of the matter is always about changing the behaviour of people'* (emphasis added).

In this chapter, bear in mind what we said in the previous chapter: behaviour change is a personal issue. Groups don't change, teams don't change, companies don't change; *individuals change*. Teams change the way they operate when each member of the team changes the way he or she operates. Companies change the way they operate when the people in them change the way they behave. Any discussion of change, even at the most general level, should never lose sight of the fact that at its heart change occurs when individuals make personal decisions about behaving differently. Andy Warhol got it right when he said, 'They always say time changes things, but you actually have to change them yourself'.

The science of behaviour change

One of the central problems with change as a field of study is that it does not have a disciplined, scientific basis. First, behaviour change is almost never measured. Behaviour is supposedly one of those things that 'just can't be measured; it's qualitative, not quantitative'. Nonsense! Behaviour *can* be measured. Continuing to ignore this fact is, as Charles Handy, the eminent thinker and writer on organizations points out, dangerous because we all know that what isn't counted doesn't count. As he says, 'If people are not counted as assets – however much we talk about them as that – but as costs, then there is every incentive to keep down those costs rather than build up those assets'.

A science must be able to do four things: describe phenomena, explain them, predict them and control them. Think of the science of ballistics as an example. It can describe the flight of a projectile, explain it, predict it and control it. That's what NASA scientists do every time they launch a rocket. Because they follow the laws of physics, very few launches fail, and when they do it is because of mechanical failure, not a change in the dynamics of propulsion and flight. The hard sciences (as opposed to the social sciences) base their principles and laws on observable, measurable data. Measurability is essential, and since it can be quite difficult to measure what you can't see (although physicists have developed very sophisticated methods of doing just that), dealing with observable phenomena, especially in a social science, is critical.

Up to now there has not been a science of behaviour change. Now there is. We call it Behaviour Kinetics. Being a scientific approach to change it concentrates only on observable, measurable data. That means it focuses purely on behaviour rather than personality because, as we pointed out in the previous chapter, you can see behaviour but you can't see personality. As far as personality goes you can only see what you believe is its manifestation – i.e. behaviour – and you infer the personality from that. You can see behaviour and therefore you can measure it. Whether personality can be measured or not is the subject of a great deal of debate.

Behaviour Kinetics is a scientific approach to behaviour change because it is able to perform the four essential functions of a science: to describe, explain, predict and control. Behaviour Kinetics is based on seven principles:

1 Behaviour drives performance.

2 The behaviour–performance link is job-specific.

3 The start point for change is acknowledgement of current behaviour.

4 The only true expert is the person who does the job.

5 Ownership of change is essential for success.

6 Change proceeds best from an AT ('ask them') approach, not a TT ('tell them') approach.

7 Successful behaviour change is based on observable, measurable data.

We addressed the first point in Chapter 1. It's what you actually *do* that makes a difference, not how you feel, think, or even how you would prefer to act. It's your behaviour that drives performance. This fact is brought home very clearly when we look at a number of people doing the same job – e.g. call-centre agents, sales people selling the same products to similar customers, waiters and waitresses in the same restaurant, etc. In all these cases some individuals perform at a higher level than others. If they have all had the same level of product and skill training, then what explains the differences in their performance? The answer is their behaviour. The A performers do things differently from the B and C performers, and close examination reveals what these things are.

> **❝ it's what you actually *do* that makes a difference ❞**

We also addressed the second point in the last chapter: that the behaviour–performance link is job-specific. Performance doesn't just result from doing things at random; it's the result of doing the right things, at the right time, in the right situation. Because the vast majority of jobs are different from one another, this means that what an individual does to achieve a high level of performance depends on what we call the behavioural demands of the job in question. Doing what is important in a specific job gets results; doing what is unimportant doesn't. The trick is to determine which behaviours are most important in any given situation and then to concentrate energy and effort on them.

So let's move on to explain the rest of the basic principles of Behaviour Kinetics.

The start point for change is acknowledgement of current behaviour

You can't improve your performance if you don't know what you are doing now. This is so obvious that people don't think about it – and that's often the root of the problem. Organizations make a clumsy attempt at addressing the issue through performance reviews, but these are generally structured around very blunt assessment tools, are often conducted long after the critical activity has taken place, and tend in many cases to be subjective. Nobody would disagree with the fact that the most effective form of performance review is continuous feedback, discussion and assessment, but for some bizarre reason managers see this as a waste of their time. So the annual review and assessment continues and everyone goes through the steps like a ritualistic rain dance. You learn the steps, you practise them every year, but they rarely produce any rain.

There is an old joke that goes something like 'If I were trying to get to . . . I wouldn't start from here'. It has a strong element of truth to it. If you're trying to get to somewhere, you need to know where you are to begin with. The literature of behaviour change is full of 'maps' that claim to show you the routes to successful change, but what they often miss out is recognizing where you are to begin with.

The starting point for any performance-related behaviour change is understanding precisely what you are currently doing. If you don't know what you're doing now, how do you know what to do differently to improve your performance? Or, as one manager so nicely put it, not knowing where you are doesn't give you a good idea of where you're heading. How we behave is often clear to others, but not necessarily clear to ourselves. People tend not to have a sharp and accurate understanding of their behaviour – how they act and what they do. Nor do they always understand the consequences of their behaviour. We all have perceptions of ourselves – of what type of person we are, of how we behave and of how we appear to others – and we base our decisions for change on these perceptions. An accurate understanding of your behaviour – the things that you do most often – is critical to making sound decisions for change. The behaviour that you exhibit frequently and consistently forms the basis for how other people see you and describe you. When asked, 'How does X manage her job?' people who work closely with the individual in question will list the various behaviours they see her using most often.

All performance improvement rests on the assumption that you know what you're currently doing. If you want to become a better presenter, then you need to know what you do now when you make presentations. If you've moved to another country and you want to make sure you pass the driving test there, you need to know how you are currently driving and what things you might be doing that will cause you to fail. Athletes generally begin their training sessions by looking at what they did last time and picking out what to correct and what to maintain. Sprinters practise their starts over and over again and constantly work on improving their running technique. Tennis players do the same sort of analysis of their techniques, shots and movements. They use video feedback because it's both objective and immediate. But it's not the video part that's important; it's the objectivity of the feedback and its immediacy. It tells them what they are doing *right now*.

Before you read any further, take a few minutes and write down the five things you do in your job that have the greatest impact on your performance. Then ask someone who works closely with you and knows you well to write down the five things they see you doing that have the greatest effect on your performance. You won't find this a particularly easy thing to do and nor will they, although it is easier for others to see our behaviour than it is for us to see it. If you are like most people, you do a lot of things without a great deal of thought. The pressure of work doesn't make it easy to take time to step back and think. However, if you want to improve your performance you need to be absolutely clear about what you're doing now, and that requires input from an objective outside source, because it's generally difficult to see yourself as clearly as others see you. Be prepared to hear some things that come as a bit of a surprise.

Why does it generally come as a shock when people give you some feedback about your behaviour? Partly it is the rarity of the experience, but also it is because we don't always realize how our actions are perceived and interpreted by others. 'Oh gosh, I didn't realize I was doing that.' People pick up the most minute and subtle things from the way others speak, move or act, yet the actors themselves generally remain oblivious of what they're doing. Have you ever wondered why sometimes when you say something nobody pays attention, but when someone else says precisely the same thing everyone latches on to it? Do you think it might have something to do with your behaviour and with the signals you're sending to people? The unfortunate thing is that unless you begin to understand what it is you're doing that causes people to ignore you, they will continue to do so. Your performance will never improve – and it certainly won't be noticed.

ᏈᏈ you need to be absolutely clear about what you're doing now ᏩᏩ

The only true expert is the person who does the job

There's unlikely to be a shortage of people in your life advising you on what you should be doing differently. Everybody is an expert on other people's lives and jobs (but unfortunately generally not on their own). However, Peter Drucker, a highly influential writer on management and organizations in the last hundred years, makes the very important point that 'One has to assume, first, that the individual human being at work knows better than anyone else what makes him or her more productive . . . even in routine work the only true expert is the person who does the job'. So if it's your job, then the person to ask about how to do it better is you. We know you may find this hard to believe. After all, if you knew what to do to improve your job performance, you'd be doing it, wouldn't you?

The problem is that while we all know, in the back of our minds, what we should be doing differently, it's exceedingly difficult to bring these thoughts and ideas up to the front of the brain and to articulate them clearly. That's why, when all else fails, it's sometimes not a bad idea to ask other people for their views on what you should be doing. They aren't encumbered with all the day-to-day distractions that make it so difficult for us to see clearly what we're doing right and what we need to do differently. But this is generally an 'all else has failed' tactic, because normally when people give us advice we don't pay attention.

The old adage is that if you want to understand someone then you need to walk a mile in their shoes. We all think we understand what other people feel, do and want, but of course we don't. All we generally do is project our own feelings, needs and solutions on to others. We don't want to walk a mile in their shoes because their shoes are the wrong size – and we weren't intending to walk in that direction anyway. So instead of really trying to understand them, which is hard work, we give them advice. Essentially we advise them to change their shoes to ones that fit our feet and to walk in the same direction as us. No wonder nobody ever listens to advice!

Finding out what you need to do differently to improve your work performance is difficult. One of the things that makes it so difficult is that not only are jobs all different from one another, but, as we've pointed out, they change all the time. It's not the same as running the 100 metres. The race is always 100 metres. The track may change slightly and the weather and the competitors may differ, but it's essentially the same every time. So as a sprinter you look at the video feedback of what you're doing, you see the various changes you need to make to improve your technique, you make them, and you evaluate the result. Simple and straightforward.

Now try that with your job (and let's assume, albeit somewhat unrealistically, that you know both exactly what you're currently doing and the results of each of your actions). Do you have any sort of blueprint for what you need to do differently? If you're lucky, your organization may have developed a set of competencies. That's a good start, but competencies are, by their nature, somewhat general. They are developed for *sets* of roles, not for each specific role and each specific job in the organization.

What else do you have? You might model your behaviour on some highly successful individual like Jack Welch or Lou Gerstner, but your job isn't the same as theirs. Or you could take the advice of various so-called gurus, consultants, colleagues or friends, but they don't really know about the intricacies of your job either. To use the slogan of the Ghostbusters, 'Who you gonna call?' The answer keeps coming up the same: you.

But as we've pointed out, it's very difficult, if not impossible, to bring the things that we know in the back of our minds up to the front of our brains in a manner that enables us to articulate precisely and specifically what we need to do to improve performance. So where does that leave us? Is there a way to get around the problem? The answer, as you might have expected, is yes. It just involves some behavioural technology, about which we will talk a bit later.

Ownership of change is essential for success

The central and most critical aspect of Behaviour Kinetics is getting individuals to take ownership of change. Without that, nothing of consequence happens. Imposing change on people never succeeds. They come to work with their brains and their egos and their emotions and their self-concepts, and they tend to do things that make them feel good about themselves, not things that satisfy the needs and objectives of someone else but do nothing for them personally. They decide what they will do differently and how they will do it.

We've discussed why we all find it difficult to accept the advice of others. Almost nobody listens to what other people tell them they should be doing. It's a behaviour pattern we have all learned well by the time we become adolescents. Parents, teachers and other authority figures are constantly telling children what they must do, and after a while it begins to grate. So we learn how to say yes but not mean it. We know people in authority are all out of touch with reality anyway, but telling them that just gets them annoyed, so it's better to pretend to go along and then do what we wanted to do in the first place.

But while we're all bad at taking advice from others, we're very good at taking our own advice. And that's why it's important for people to have ownership of change; by which we mean that the decision to do something differently belongs to the individual, not to some other person, be it boss, colleague, parent, or whoever. Basically, if it's your own idea to do something, you'll do it; if it's someone else's idea being pushed down your throat, you'll resist it.

What should you do differently in order to improve your job performance? Start by going back to the list you made earlier of the five most important things that you are currently doing. Let's define those as successful behaviours. After all, they are the things that have got you to where you are today in your job, so unless things are going really badly for you, a number of them must be right. (And if things are going badly for you, they are clearly not the right behaviours on which to focus your effort and energy. So all the more reason to start thinking about what you should be doing differently.)

Now think of three things (start with just three) that you are doing that are not bringing about the results you would hope for or expect. Let's define those as *un*successful behaviours. What's different about these things? Why aren't they producing desired results for you? What's getting in the way? What can you do about these obstacles? If you look at what makes your successful behaviours successful, is there a pattern? When you look at the three behaviours that are not working for you, is there a different pattern? Just going through this simple (but not necessarily easy) process will start to get you focused on the performance–behaviour link in your particular job. It's not as slick and sharp as using behavioural technology, but it will take you some distance down the right path.

Change proceeds best from an AT approach, not a TT approach

We know that it's you that decides whether you are going to change your behaviour, but how do you get other people to change theirs? Certainly not by giving them advice or telling them what to do! They're no different from you. They think their ideas are great, but they're not so sure about yours. They need to own their own ideas for change every bit as much as you do. So how do you help people take ownership of behaviour change? You have to adopt what we call an AT ('ask them') approach and stop using a TT ('tell them') approach.

If you are a manager you're probably not liking the way this is going. What do we mean, asking people what they think they should be doing? Surely a manager is paid to know what people should be doing, and for getting them to do it. Otherwise why are they managers? You can't just leave everyone to do whatever they think because it would result in chaos. There has to be some supervision, some coordination, some integration, some leadership.

Yes there does, but let us repeat Peter Drucker's observation: 'One has to assume, first, that the individual human being at work knows better than anyone else what makes him or her more productive . . . even in routine work the only true expert is the person who does the job'. So how can we allow people the freedom to decide what should be done to improve their performance and at the same time be able to coordinate what they're doing with the overall objectives of the business? The answer is to blend the input of individuals with the objectives and requirements of the organization, and to do so in as flexible and open a manner as possible. In case this sounds as though it's becoming fuzzy and impractical, let's take a look at an outstanding example of how the process works. It's Toyota.

Toyota charges every employee – assembly line workers, sales staff, service engineers, people in accounting, HR, IT, at every level and in every function – with the responsibility to improve their processes and their productivity, and to find innovative ways to satisfy their internal customers and the company's customers. The company's 'Toyota Way' document says, 'We strive to decide our own fate. We act with self-reliance, trusting in our own abilities. We accept responsibility for our conduct and for maintaining and improving the skills that enable us to produce added value.' And that applies to *everyone* from, as they describe it, top-level executives 'up to' the workers on the shop floor. Everyone is expected and encouraged to suggest better ways of doing things.

In the 1980s, Toyota received over half a million suggestions a year from its employees about how to do things better – suggestions for everything from how to keep the floors clean to how to solve an engineering problem. The average was about 12 suggestions per employee per year.

> **" everyone is expected and encouraged to suggest better ways of doing things "**

The number is now many, many times that. But the most interesting thing is that Toyota's management accepted and implemented 85–90 percent of those suggestions. The same thing has been happening in Toyota ever since. As a result, it is now the second largest car manufacturer in the world. Its market capitalization is more than the big three (General Motors, Ford and Chrysler) put together and greater than its Japanese rivals, Honda and Nissan, combined. The Lexus is recognized as the best engineered car in the world. Toyotas at every level are the benchmark for quality for the automobile industry. By almost any yardstick, Toyota is the world's most successful automotive company. It didn't get that way by accident. It did it by giving its people ownership of change – by asking them what they thought they needed to do differently to improve their performance and the performance of the company, and then implementing their ideas.

In the 1950s General Motors had a market share of almost 60 percent in the USA. It now has a share of a little more than a third of that. Working in one of the GM car divisions in the late 1960s we saw no sign of any way a non-managerial employee could make a suggestion. The accepted wisdom was that GM engineers (from GM's own college of engineering, The General Motors Institute) knew how to make a car, and the job of the assembly plant people was to put it together. The message was clear: don't bother making any suggestions. End of story. GM was a pure TT culture, just as Toyota is a pure AT culture. So for 50 years GM has been going down the path of TT and it has continued to lose market share; its credit has been downgraded so that its bonds are junk status; it is losing money hand over fist; and because it seems incapable of seeing that its approach to management is wrong, it is blaming the unions for its plight. Toyota, on the other hand, has been going down the AT path and has quietly overtaken everyone else in the industry. It will soon be bigger than GM. Rick Wagoner, the CEO of GM, recently remarked, 'The key thing is to remember what you've learned so you don't have to relearn it'. Let's hope he meant it.

More than 50 years of research and example has shown that when people are allowed to take responsibility for changing their behaviour, they do; and when change is imposed on them, they resist. Fifty years! How long does it take to learn the lesson? Managers still try to impose change on their people without consultation or involvement, and they are still amazed when it doesn't work very well. They put it down to people being obstinate, stupid or lazy, but they never apply these adjectives to themselves. 'Ask them, don't tell them' should be a framed motto on every manager's desk.

Successful behaviour change is based on observable, measurable data

To improve performance it is necessary to focus on the observable things people do – their *behaviours*. Note the use of the plural. We are talking not about people's styles, but about the *specific* things they do, the actions they take, the decisions they make. One of the problems with the concept of style – leadership style, management style, behavioural style – is that style descriptions look and sound rather like descriptions of personality type. For instance, here is a style description from a well-known leadership model: 'People-oriented, motivator, builds personal relationships, likeable, interpersonal skills, cares for others'. And here's a personality description from a widely used personality profiling instrument: 'Warm-hearted, talkative, popular, conscientious, born cooperator, always doing something nice for someone'. Is there any difference?

If you look at the leadership style description again you'll see that it describes personality traits, not behaviours. 'People-oriented' describes an attitude or value, but what *behaviours* need to be exhibited to demonstrate people-orientation? The same is true of 'motivator'. What does that mean in terms of actual behaviour? Many things can be motivating. So which of these does this individual demonstrate?

One of the immediate problems with style descriptions is that they lack clear definition – i.e. they are not openly observable and measurable. What do we mean by something like 'being directive'? What are the specific behaviours that make up directiveness? Does being directive mean telling people what to do? Not listening to people? Holding inflexible opinions? Bullying people? Is it all of the above or some of the above? How do you identify when someone is being less directive or more directive? If you wish to change the level of directive behaviour that you or someone else is using, you have to be able to identify examples of *specific*, *describable* and *measurable* directive actions. It is not good enough to state the change goal as 'to be less directive'. You need to know specifically what has to be done differently, and you need to be able to measure it. Style descriptions are helpful, but they are general pictures of a set of behaviours, and they are not able to separate out which of the behaviours in the set make a difference and which don't. This is critically important.

For example, having an objective to 'cut down on smoking' is meaningless unless you define by how much and when. First you need to know how many cigarettes you are currently smoking per day (the start point). Then you need to define the desired end point. If you don't define a clear end point, then how can you measure achievement? If the start point is 40 cigarettes per day, is 38 per day 'cutting down'? Obviously yes, but it's of so little consequence as to make no difference. What's the goal? Ten per day? By when? By next week, the week after, the week after that? Measurement of observable behaviour is critical for change to take place.

❝ measurement of observable behaviour is critical for change to take place ❞

Behaviour can be measured in terms of its frequency and its intensity. If someone tells you that you shout at people, you need to find out two things. First you need to ask for specific examples of the frequency of the behaviour – when you've shouted at someone over the past 30 days, for example. Then you need to have the intensity of your shouting described on some sort of scale. Did you scream at high volume? Did you raise your voice so you could be heard 5 metres away? Or did you raise your voice noticeably above its normal level, but only to the extent that it would carry about 2 metres?

Frequency of behaviour is important. Having raised your voice to someone twice in the last 30 days is clearly not the same as having done it 15 times. There is a range of about 300–400 different specific behaviours that people exhibit in a work situation. Most of us do most of these things, but we only do a few of them a lot of the time. Given a list of 100 behaviours and asked whether they have done these things, individuals will generally tick 95 percent of them. When they're asked which of them they do *often*, the number drops to 20 or less. Even at this most subjective and highly imprecise level, this measurement is very useful. It starts to show people what they do to drive their performance. Research shows that the 20 or so things that an individual does in the management of their job account for more than 80 percent of the results they achieve. The rest of the things we do have little or no impact on performance.

If you are shooting on a rifle range, a critical element in the process is being able to see, after each shot, where you hit the target so you can make whatever adjustments are necessary to get closer to the bull's-eye. When you shoot for the first time with a new rifle, you begin by taking a few 'sighting shots' – i.e. you shoot and see what happens. On the basis of the results, you make some adjustments in order to improve your performance. You start off by seeing the consequences of your initial actions and you immediately adjust your behaviour on the basis of that information. You are able to improve your performance when, shortly after you do something, you get observable and measurable data-based feedback on your behaviour and its results.

Performance improvement requires that you know what you are doing now, and specifically what it is that you're doing that is driving results. Performance measures are often defined with some degree of rigour. One of the driving forces behind the rigour is that remuneration is either based on performance or is at least supposed to be based on performance. Attention moves to where the money is. But while the output/results end of the performance issue gets lots of attention, very little attention is paid to the input/behaviour end.

At its worst, this focus on ends and not means can lead to unethical and criminal practices. Over the last few years there have been some of the most astoundingly brazen cases of fraud and misrepresentation. But even at its best, focusing purely on the end result and not paying any heed to how people get there means that in many cases results are a matter of trial and error. If you don't know which of your actions have a significant and direct effect on your performance, you are reduced to doing things on the basis of hunch, guess, or the assumption that what has worked in the past will continue to work in the future. Sometimes it does, but increasingly, as the pace of change continues to accelerate, it doesn't.

At a corporate level, the world of business is littered with companies that have disappeared from the face of the earth because they failed to see change occurring and didn't adjust to it in time. It's easy to find dozens upon dozens of examples, because they get written up in the media. But the tens of thousands of individuals who fall prey to the same errors of failing to adjust their behaviour to changing circumstances don't get any coverage, although a number of your former colleagues, neighbours and friends are among them. To avoid joining them, make sure you understand exactly what you're doing to drive performance. That's the first step to survival, and the first step to success.

The need for behavioural technology

Certain pieces of data are essential to Behaviour Kinetics: identifying precisely, in terms of a list of specific individual behaviours, what people are doing now; and identifying what they need to do differently, also in terms of a list of specific behaviours. Even though Behaviour Kinetics relies on an AT approach, neither of these critical pieces of information can be obtained simply by asking people, 'What are you doing now, and what should you be doing differently to improve your performance?' The fact of the matter is that nobody can provide adequate answers. We simply don't have the vocabulary or the cognitive mapping required to generate detailed and accurate answers to these questions. *However, we do know the answers.*

People need to have a clear, objective and accurate benchmark of their current behaviour upon which to build their strategy for performance improvement. And they need to have a clear and detailed behavioural map that guides them to change their behaviour in such a manner that improves performance results. Unfortunately, there is no way to get either of these things without the application of behavioural technology. It is a principal objective of this book to stimulate the further development of this technology. There are currently a number of behavioural diagnostics available in the marketplace and Part 2 of the book provides examples of several of them. They vary in sophistication and focus, but they all try to address the fundamental questions that underlie performance improvement: 'What are you doing now?' and 'What do you need to do differently to improve your performance?'

Chapter summary

One of the problems with change as a field of study is that it does not have a disciplined, scientific basis. A science is able to do four things: describe phenomena, explain them, predict them and control them. Change is rarely described clearly, more rarely explained clearly, and almost never predicted or controlled. Behaviour Kinetics is a scientific approach to change that attempts to engage these issues. It is based on seven principles:

1 Behaviour drives performance.

2 The behaviour–performance link is job-specific.

3 The start point for change is acknowledgement of current behaviour.

4 The only true expert is the person who does the job.

5 Ownership of change is essential for success.

6 Change proceeds best from an AT ('ask them') approach, not a TT ('tell them') approach.

7 Successful behaviour change is based on observable, measurable data.

Performance improvement is based on observable, measurable data. The starting point for any performance improvement is understanding precisely (observable, measurable behaviour) what you are doing currently. How can you change your behaviour if you are not clear about what you're doing now, and especially what you're doing that makes a difference and what doesn't? But once you know what you're doing currently and the results of your actions, the next thing is to work out what you need to do differently. For this you need the help of some behavioural technology that gives you an answer in specific behaviour terms. Style descriptions are helpful, but they are general pictures of a set of behaviours, and they are not able to separate out which of the behaviours in the set make a difference and which don't. This is critically important.

Change is an individual decision. Organizational change begins with individuals changing how they behave, and deciding what they will or won't do. People generally resist being told what to do. They can accept some direction but tend to bridle at too much of it. We all like our own ideas and we generally like them more than the ideas and suggestions of other people. Because ownership of change is so important, it works best when it is based on an 'ask them' (AT) approach rather than the far more common 'tell them' (TT) approach. The proof is the consistently outstanding performance over decades of Toyota, the classic example of an AT company. In contrast, General Motors has, since its inception, been a TT company and has seen its market share and profitability steadily erode over the past 40 years.

3

Be a leader, not a celebrity

Vision is not enough. It must be combined with venture. It is not enough to stare up the steps, we must step up the stairs.
(Vaclav Havel)

Leadership is about getting people to improve their performance. When groups of people achieve things, it's the leader who generally gets credited with having brought them to their level of performance. In sport, when a team performs poorly it's the manager or coach who gets fired. In the corporate world, when companies perform badly shareholders call for the scalp of the CEO. A high-profile example is Carly Fiorina, fired from her job as CEO of Hewlett-Packard. The reasons given were the performance of HP's stock, which fell in value by 55 percent over the length of her tenure. However, the cautionary title of this chapter also appears to resonate behind the downfall. In 1998 *Fortune* magazine named her America's most powerful businesswoman, apologising at the time that she was 'someone you've never heard of'. But from then on she was someone we heard of all the time. Patience Wheatcroft in *The Times* remarked that 'During her five and a half years running the business, Ms Fiorina had become a star of the international business scene . . . But what the board of HP has decided [is] that it needs someone to pay close attention to things back at the ranch.'

Leadership has unfortunately become a cult thing. People in leadership positions have achieved celebrity status. The names of the princes of industry roll off the tongue almost as easily as the names of the star athletes or actors of the day. These are the people who, we are told, make things happen. But as Jim Collins remarks, 'To use an analogy, the "Leadership is the answer to everything" perspective is the modern equivalent of the "God is the answer to everything" perspective that held back our scientific understanding of the physical world in the Dark Ages'. There are literally thousands of articles and hundreds of books written about leadership every year. But many of the people who write them wouldn't know leadership if they sat on it. Be careful of fads. If it seems too good/easy to be true, it probably is.

The media is full of stories about the lives of the rich and famous and these days many of these rich and famous are corporate executives. Compensation for senior executives has risen out of all proportion. According to *The New York Times*, in 2003 the average CEO of a major US company received $9.2 million in total compensation. The average Fortune 500 chief executive made 530 times more than the average person working in the company. William McDonough, chairman of the Public Accounting Oversight Board in the USA, remarked in testimony before the US Congress: 'There is no economic theory on God's planet that can justify that'.

That's not the type of leadership we're talking about in this book. The fact is that you don't have to be at the top of your organization to be a leader. You don't have to be a manager to be a leader. Leadership takes place everywhere. Once you understand that leadership is about performance improvement – getting things done well, done better, done faster, done on time, done reliably – then you realize that everyone in an organization has a leadership role to play, and that the old concept that there are a few leaders and a lot of followers no longer applies.

The 'great man' theory of leadership

Much of what you hear and read about leadership is based on the idea of the 'great man' theory. This is the idea that if you study the lives of great leaders – corporate, military or political – you can identify the qualities that differentiate them from ordinary people and hence discover the characteristics that you should develop to become a leader yourself. The theory goes hand in hand with the misguided belief that leaders are born, not made, and it's nonsense.

But the myth dies hard. In his book *The Apprentice*, Sir Alan Sugar states, 'Leaders tend to be born rather than made'. Hopefully people who read the book will pay no attention to that remark. Stephen Overell in an article in the *Financial Times* entitled 'To hell with great men' commented:

As with history, the study of leadership has suffered at the hands of Great Men. The image of the CEO as hero, glistening with steely determination and charisma, remains an enduring one that no amount of fraud, share option scams or plain reality has managed to dislodge. If leadership is all about individual magnetism, not a lot more can be said. You either have it or you don't.

So if you don't have it, then no amount of reading or training courses or development is going to change things – and Sir Alan's not going to sell many of his books, because people who are born leaders don't need to read it and it's a waste of time for those who aren't.

In about 500 BC, Confucius travelled around China trying to persuade the various feudal kings of the time that he had the formula for effective leadership – an early great man theory that proposed a set of traits and characteristics that would make a king a successful leader. His view was that a leader had to be benevolent, humane, just and moderate. The first emperor of China, Ch'in Shih Huang Ti, made his opinion about this theory pretty clear by having 460 Confucian monks buried alive or buried up to their necks and decapitated.

So never mind great men and forget about lists of magical traits that turn people into leaders. The fact is that all behaviour is learned, and leadership behaviour is no exception.

** all behaviour is learned, and leadership behaviour is no exception**

Leadership is about behaviour, not personality traits. The personalities of the individuals whom *Fortune* rates as being the six most powerful business leaders in the world – Lee Scott, Warren Buffett, Bill Gates, Jeff Immelt, Rupert Murdoch and Michael Dell – are completely different from one another. (In fact you probably don't know who Lee Scott is, and he's ranked number one. He's the CEO of Wal-Mart, the number one company on the Fortune 500.) Great men come in all kinds of shapes, sizes and personalities – and they aren't all men. How about Abby Johnson (Fidelity funds) and Meg Whitman (eBay), both of whom make it into the top 25 most powerful business leaders? It's not their personality that has made them great leaders, it's their *behaviour* – what they *do*.

In his book *Good to Great*, Jim Collins summarizes research that took him and his team 10.5 people years of work. They analyzed the results of 1,435 companies over a period from 1965 to 1995, examined 6,000 articles, and generated over 2,000 pages of interview transcripts. One of their major conclusions is that 'Larger-than-life, celebrity leaders . . . are negatively correlated with taking a company from good to great'.

A corollary to the great man theory is what might be called the 'right person at the right time' theory. Abigail Adams, wife of John Adams, the first vice-president of the USA and its second president, coined a popular saying when she wrote to Thomas Jefferson 'Great necessities call forth great leaders'. That might be interpreted to mean that people become leaders when they are able to channel their behaviour to handle great necessities, to learn from them, and to develop the skills and behaviour necessary to deal with them. However, it has more often been taken to mean that it is really just the event that causes born leaders to, like Superman, strip off their outer clothing to reveal the marvellous individual hidden beneath the humble exterior.

The fact is that leadership is about what people *do*, not what people are. Titles may confer leadership roles but only behaviour produces leadership. Being a chief executive only says that an individual has the job, not that they can do it well. Stephen Overell was right: to hell with great men.

What is leadership?

If you're experiencing difficulty sleeping, a sure cure for your insomnia is to read through a list of the definitions of leadership. Academics, few of whom have ever exhibited any leadership themselves, and ever fewer of whom have ever worked in organizations where leadership is a core component of success, have created a leadership industry. At the last count there were upwards of 500 definitions of leadership. Pick up a management textbook and work your way through the various theories of leadership being 'researched'. If you can get through them with any real grasp of what leadership is, you will have achieved something quite remarkable.

But this isn't a textbook and there won't be any listing of theories of leadership. This book is about fact – scientifically proven fact. People exhibit leadership by the things they do and say. Leadership implies getting people to change their behaviour and either do different things, or do things differently. But what is it that leaders do that gets others to act differently? The answer is that they do and say things that are appropriate to the situation at hand. The effectiveness of leadership behaviour is a direct result of the degree to which it reflects the demands of the situation. Winston Churchill was a magnificent wartime leader who made millions of people focus their behaviour in different ways in order to conquer a common enemy. But when the war had ended and the situation was very different, Churchill was no longer the man for the time and was resoundingly voted out of office.

Leadership is about improving people's performance and performance is judged by results. Therefore leadership must be judged by results. Everything you do has the potential to influence the behaviour of others. Your leadership can therefore be judged by both what you do and what you influence others to do. It's about behaviour and behaviour change.

As a result of our conversations with more than 5,000 managers we know that the things leaders do either have the effect of accelerating performance, sustaining performance or blocking performance. Every action has an effect. As Niall Fitzgerald, chairman of Reuters, remarked, 'One of the things that leaders don't fully recognize is that when they speak or act they are speaking into an extraordinary amplification system'. Every action causes people to do something. People pay attention to what leaders do and say and they adjust their behaviour accordingly, either to accelerate performance levels, to sustain and maintain performance, or hinder performance.

The hard facts about leadership

After the Second World War the US government sponsored a massive piece of research into leadership. The experience of the war showed that officer selection boards were notoriously inefficient at determining individuals' leadership abilities. Despite the fact that they had all gone through essentially the same process of selection (and completed the same personality tests), some officers ended up with brilliant leadership records while others were dismal failures. Clearly the underlying assumption that had been made prior to the selection procedure was that leaders are born not made. The objective of the process, therefore, was to determine who 'had it' and who didn't.

When it turned out that the basic assumption underlying the process was flawed, the US government agreed to fund research to find out what did, in fact, determine leadership effectiveness. When the researchers had spent roughly half a million dollars examining the behaviour of a large number of officers, they concluded that leadership was comprised of two types of behaviour: the degree to which an individual focuses their behaviour on tasks (taking action, getting the job done, getting results) or focuses behaviour on building and maintaining relationships (showing concern for people, aiding them in their development, being sensitive to interpersonal needs, etc.).

That makes some sense. We've all known people who are very strongly task-oriented but not interpersonally skilled. We've also known individuals who work well with, and display a genuine interest in, people but don't really show much interest in results. And of course we've all known people who do both these things, and some who appear to do very little of either.

But there is a third, critical element of leadership behaviour. Rick Roskin, a Canadian management writer, researcher, consultant and academic, and a man who has rarely been one to take accepted theory as accepted, has done a lot of work on leadership, and his conclusions are supported by the 5,000 managers to whom we talked. Roskin observed that there is more to leadership than simply going hammer and tongs at getting things done, and/or focusing all your energies on people, relationships and interpersonal growth. One of the things that makes leadership as difficult as it is, is the ability to coordinate activities, pull diverse outputs together, integrate processes and results, and see the bigger picture. The third major element of a leader's job is about integrating and coordinating things. Leaders do this by implementing processes, procedures and systems.

So we have three basic approaches to leadership: *action* (initiating activities, driving for results, getting things done by dint of personal effort); *people* (showing concern for people, aiding them in their development, being sensitive to interpersonal needs and relationships); and something that we might call *system* (coordination of activities, integration of outputs, strategic thinking and action). The trick is deciding what combination of the three best fits the situation.

The fit between preference and situation

From the 1950s (when they first entered the market) until the1980s, televisions were not overly reliable. As a result, the TV rental business came into being and grew rapidly. One of the biggest players in the UK was Granada. It had major market share and shops in virtually every high street in the UK. It was also, under its outstanding managing director Bill Edwardes, highly efficient and very profitable. The business was essentially system driven. Granada TV Rental knew the location of every TV it rented, it knew whether rental payments were up to date, it knew how many TVs were under repair, how many were being replaced, its costs, its revenues and its profits. It was an exceptionally well-run company that made very healthy profits.

In the mid-1980s the TV rental business began to change. TV sets became more reliable and durable. The advantage of renting a set and thereby being assured of no problems and no breakdowns began to disappear. TVs no longer broke down so often. They lasted for years and years and performed flawlessly. And they became cheaper. So the board of Granada TV Rental began a strategic assessment of the business and began to look at alternatives. One alternative that was considered was to move into the retail electronic goods market, selling TVs, radios, stereos, and the whole range of household electronic products. It already had absolutely prime retail locations in every centre of any size in the UK and it had a strong customer base about whom it knew quite a lot. Retail electronics looked like a good option. However, the executive board rightly decided against it. The reason was that the behaviour that defined the culture of Granada TV Rental was oriented to system, while the behaviour required to compete on the high street in retail is much more action-oriented. In the highly competitive retail business, products, prices and promotions can change almost daily. Flexibility and risk taking are prerequisites for success. Granada TV Rental was solid, systematic, focused, and very good at its business, but flexibility and risk taking were not part of the equation.

Are there only a few leaders in any organization?

If you think you're too small to have an impact, try going to bed with a mosquito in the room. (Anita Roddick)

Leadership is not just limited to managers, nor is it the sole responsibility of the people at the top. Individuals at all levels exert influence over the behaviour of others – and that's what leadership is about. Everyone in an organization can be, and should be, a leader in some way or other. The idea that there are leaders and followers has a variety of damaging consequences. First, it alows so-called leaders to believe that they, and only they, know what should be done and how to do it. Second, it encourages so-called followers to abdicate responsibility – 'It's not my fault; it's not my responsibility. I have no control over things; I just do what I'm told.' And that's nonsense. Make the outcomes important and you soon see whether people really exert no initiative and just do what they're told. Anyone who's been in a combat situation in the army knows that every individual has a leadership role of one kind or another. The results of the cattle-drive mentality of the idiot commanders of the First World War are horrible and powerful reminders of where the leaders-and-followers model takes us.

There is a lot of talk about the difference between leadership and management. It arises from the cult of leadership, which seeks to elevate those it anoints with the title of leader to heights above normal human beings. (And if you think we're exaggerating, pick up almost any book about leadership and look at the language that is lavished on the descriptions of leaders.) Differentiating between leaders and managers tends to imply that managers aren't leaders – i.e. that what they do does not influence people to do things differently, does not impact on performance, and does not focus on results. Clearly that is nonsense. 'Manager' is a term that is applied to an individual in a supervisory role in an organization. Managers manage people and/or tasks, and in both instances their management activity is expected to produce some sort of results. Managers are assessed on their performance, just like everyone else. They are as interested in improving their performance as anyone else. And they certainly exert influence over what other people do, whether wittingly or unwittingly. What they do meets the essential criterion of leadership – influencing people to improve their performance and achieve results.

British Leyland, once upon a time the British equivalent of General Motors or Ford, produced famous brands of cars – Jaguar, Rover, Land Rover, Triumph, Austin, MG, and Morris. Its demise can be entirely attributed to staggeringly bad management, one indication of which was the very clear demarcation between management and workers. Leadership was seen as something only managers could provide, and the more senior the manager the greater their alleged leadership skills (and *alleged* is the operative word). For instance, Jaguar in the early 1970s produced fewer that 40,000 cars over the length of a year. To get an idea of how trivial this level of production is, it represents about two or three days of what a major automobile manufacturer turns out. However, despite the fact that it was small and rather insignificant, Jaguar had separate dining rooms for directors, for senior managers, for managers and for supervisors. And then there was the canteen for the workers! When Niall Fitzgerald talks about managers' actions being broadcast through a huge amplification system, he's not exaggerating. Workers at Jaguar got the message very loud and very clear. And so they reacted to it by turning a great brand into something synonymous with poor quality and shoddy workmanship. It was only when Sir John Egan became chairman and chief executive and both demonstrated and encouraged real leadership that the situation was turned around and the company acquired some value.

Management in the rest of the Leyland empire was no better. The great Austin-Morris and Triumph-Rover factories in and around Oxford and Birmingham were run by people who thought they were leaders because they had titles and wore ties, and who thought that front-line employees had nothing to offer. However, leadership skills are widely distributed throughout the population. Front-line workers can show every bit as much leadership as managers, only they often channel it into different areas. In Toyota much of it is channelled into making the company more successful. In British Leyland it was channelled into militant unionism and sabotage. The car plants became a battleground in the class war. Performance-blocking behaviour, which we shall discuss at some length in this book, was rife. Quality disappeared. The company eventually suffered the consequences and disappeared from the face of the earth.

Performance-sustaining leadership

There are some subtle but important differences in the focus of leadership. The type of leadership with which we are most familiar is a focus on accelerating performance – moving things forward, creating change, driving a vision, constantly improving results. But like an army advancing rapidly across territory and successively engaging the enemy as it moves forward, without a myriad of support systems to sustain the advance everything soon grinds to a dismal halt. The word to focus on here is *sustain*. One of the roles of leadership is to ensure that certain performance levels are sustained, that certain systems and processes are maintained, and that things like quality, customer satisfaction and profitability remain consistent. Only when there is a stable base is it possible to move forward. An army requires maintenance of its transport, its arms and its equipment. A company requires maintenance of its production systems, its accounting systems and its logistical systems. It's no use being able to make the very best widget in the world at the very best price if you can't deliver it and get paid for it. It's no use developing better and better widgets if you can't produce them with consistent quality. Sustaining performance in certain areas is critical.

Sustaining performance requires a specialized form of leadership. It is perhaps best described as stewardship behaviour. *The Oxford Dictionary* defines a steward as 'a person whose responsibility it is to take care of something'. Note that there is no mention of *changing* the something, doing the something differently, or of creating a new something. A steward's focus is on sustaining performance, making sure things are dealt with properly, that they run smoothly and that there are no hiccups. Stewardship evokes images of safe hands, consistency, smooth running and no surprises. It's a very important element of leadership.

££ only when there is a stable base is it possible to move forward 55

Holiday Inns used to use the slogan 'No surprises' in its marketing. Its aim was to take the anxiety out of selecting a hotel for either business or personal travel. The slogan ensured consistency. It neither promised the grand 'wow' experience or the heart dropping 'oh no' experience. It promised comfort, familiarity and reliability. That's what competent performance-sustaining leadership delivers. It makes sure things run as they should, that products get delivered on time, that payment is collected on time, that quality is maintained, that regulations are complied with, and so on. It makes people both inside and outside the organization feel comfortable and secure. No organization can survive without a significant degree of performance-sustaining behaviour. All the outwardly glamorous and exciting businesses of the world, like investment banking, advertising, movies, fashion design, etc., have 'back office' teams that manage all the processes and administrative bits and pieces that make sure the financial deals are completed, the media campaigns are distributed and the fashion shows are presented.

Performance-sustaining leadership is directed towards improving efficiency, getting things done right, ensuring that systems and processes operate optimally, giving people adequate skills and maintaining quality. It focuses on optimizing results with given resources. It aims to make the organization as efficient as possible, to ensure clear goals and objectives, to maintain consistency, to achieve more with less, to treat people properly, to run a tight ship. It gets on with doing what needs to be done – with existing people, existing budgets and existing facilities.

This is a type of leadership that is almost never talked about. We read about people like Jeff Immelt, Bill Gates and Rupert Murdoch, but we seldom hear about the hundreds and thousands of people in their companies who actually make things run, who actually make the money, collect the money, spend the money, deliver the product or service, and deal with the customers. The cult of leadership would have you believe that the performance of an organization is due to one or two individuals, and that without these magnificent super-heroes the company would fall into the abyss. The fact is that without competent stewardship the company would long ago have imploded, regardless of the powers of the super-heroes.

Research demonstrates how important performance-sustaining behaviour is to the success of a company. In an article in the *Harvard Business Review*, Michael Mankins and Richard Steele summarized a study undertaken in 2004 in collaboration with The Economist Intelligence Unit in which they surveyed senior executives from 197 companies worldwide with sales in excess of $500 million, exploring how successfully their corporations were at translating strategy into performance. The findings were highly revealing. They found that on average almost 30 percent of performance was lost due to inadequate levels of performance-sustaining behaviour.

Mankins and Steele's analysis reveals that what happens is roughly the following. Strategy is formulated but communicated poorly. Hence, quite logically, there is considerable difficulty in determining how to translate strategy into specific actions and behaviours – if you are not clear what the strategy is, inevitably you are not going to be clear how to implement it and what resources will be needed – where, when, and to do what. Confusion results and performance failure is compounded by not clarifying objectives and allocating clear responsibility for them. Performance is not monitored; success is not rewarded; failure has no consequences; resources are not allocated appropriately; and people aren't provided with necessary skills and capabilities.

Results from the 197 companies surveyed indicate that breakdowns in planning and execution account for a total performance loss of 37 percent between setting a strategy and implementing it. Of this 37 percent, 25 percent can be directly attributed to inadequate levels of performance-sustaining leadership behaviour. Mankins and Steele provide a detailed breakdown of where the performance loss occurs. The causes specifically related to lack of performance-sustaining behaviour are:

▪ *Inadequate or unavailable resources – 7.5 percent.* Having appropriate resources does not necessarily accelerate performance, but not having them certainly hinders it.

▪ *Poorly communicated strategy – 5.2 percent.* General communication is an organizational lubricant; without decent communication things go off the rails. Anyone who's ever been in the army in a battle situation, real or simulated, knows how essential communication is for survival, let alone victory. Business is a battleground; the only difference is that injuries are psychological rather than physical, but the former can be as painful as the latter.

▪ *Actions required to execute not clearly defined – 4.5 percent.* Execution and vision are two quite different things. Vision accelerates performance, but only if it is implemented by a myriad of unglamorous, unexciting, often repetitive, basic actions and decisions. The top of the stairs is the vision, but you need to go up them one by one to achieve it.

▪ *Unclear accountabilities for execution – 4.1 percent.* Clear definition of responsibility is something that is central to all business success. Defining responsibility does not necessarily accelerate performance, but not defining it puts the organization up to its knees in molasses.

▪ *Inadequate performance monitoring – 3.0 percent.* What gets measured gets done. Without measurement, actions and results show a tendency to randomness.

▪ *Inadequate skills and capabilities – 0.7 percent.* Like physical and financial resources, appropriate and adequate skills and capabilities help accelerate performance, but lack of them obstructs it.

Performance-sustaining leadership is vital to a company. When it fails, the company performs poorly, or, in the extreme case, expires.

Performance-accelerating leadership

Performance-accelerating leadership is about behaviour that is directed towards improving effectiveness, driving changes and improvements, taking the offensive against competitors, creating vision and direction, generating excitement and commitment, inspiring a winning culture, ensuring that systems and processes operate optimally, and increasing returns. Its focus is to add value by doing things differently and better. It constantly questions existing systems, existing structures and existing assumptions, and existing ways of operating.

While performance-sustaining behaviour focuses on what to do on the journey, performance-accelerating behaviour focuses on where to go. Performance-sustaining leadership behaviour reflects the maintenance of efficient systems and practices, consistency, and guarding stakeholder value. Performance-accelerating behaviour is managing the changing, the unknown and the unpredictable. It requires vision and the ability to get people to go where they have not countenanced going before. It is leadership behaviour that is focused on changing things and doing things differently. It is about making a difference and challenging the status quo.

Performance-accelerating leadership tends to be seen as glamorous because newness and change are often more glitzy than regularity and stability. But driving changes – taking the offensive, creating a vision and generating excitement – never made anyone a penny unless they could also deliver. Planning on its own is a waste of time; planning followed by execution delivers results. Carly Fiorina was fired not for lack of vision and drive, but for lack of execution. Her successor at Hewlett-Packard, Mark Hurd, who *Business Week* called the 'Un-Carly', is not making the same mistake. He is doing things like changing the sales force from generalists to specific product experts who can deliver against the product-focused salespeople from competitors like Dell and Lexmark.

The balance of behaviour

Leadership is about influencing people's performance. It's about behaviour and behaviour change. But it's also about balance – the balance between performance-accelerating leadership and performance-sustaining leadership. Using the analogy of a car, there is a balance that must be achieved between accelerating and sustaining movement. You cannot accelerate indefinitely because that will simply spin the car out of control and blow the engine. And there are various systems in the car that must be kept performing properly – the fuel feed, the valves and pistons, the transmission, the steering mechanism, the suspension, the brakes, etc. These are essential to maintain the car's movement. The accelerator is only applied when it's necessary to pass another vehicle, or to go faster. The same is true of organizations. Competitive pressures, technological developments and customer demands require the organization constantly to improve performance in certain areas. But at the same time consistency must be maintained in the management of inventories, supply chains, receivables, staffing, quality and a host of other areas.

> **there is a balance that must be achieved between accelerating and sustaining movement**

The balance of performance-accelerating and performance-sustaining leadership behaviour is critical for success both for individuals and organizations:

■ too much performance-accelerating leadership behaviour and not enough performance-sustaining behaviour results in loss of control and confusion;

■ too much performance-sustaining behaviour and not enough performance-accelerating behaviour results in complacency and stagnation.

The cult of leadership would of course disagree with this. They would argue that you can't have too much vision, you can't be too inspiring, change is always necessary because the world is constantly changing, and you can't take too much initiative or set too much of an out-front example. But what if it ain't broke? Do you have to, as the management guru Tom Peters advises, break it anyway? Does leadership always have to be exercised from the front, flags waving and bugles sounding? Darwin Smith didn't think so, and nor did the rest of the great leaders Jim Collins talks about whose performance outstripped their industries and the markets consistently for over 15 consecutive years.

Can an organization have too much performance-accelerating behaviour? The answer is yes, and here's an example. The president of a technology company we know lost his job not because he wasn't an inspirational leader or because he didn't surround himself with people who subscribed to a common vision and drove change forward, but because he didn't make sure the company had enough people focusing on performance-sustaining behaviour. His behaviour was focused very strongly on accelerating performance, and so was the behaviour of his team and the teams below them. The company was growing like wildfire, expanding its markets, gaining market share and increasing revenues. They were a darling of the markets – until they reported incorrect figures for the company's performance not once but three times in short succession. The market overlooked the first mistake because it was quickly dealt with, very grudgingly forgave the second, but lost its patience at the third. To repeat, too much performance-accelerating behaviour and not enough performance-sustaining behaviour results in loss of control and confusion.

On the other hand, too great a focus on performance-sustaining behaviour and not enough on performance-accelerating behaviour results in complacency and stagnation. A company specializing in fast-moving consumer goods (FMCG) failed to adapt its products to changing consumer preferences, became bogged down in process, failed to implement new technology, and failed to improve productivity. It experienced a dramatic fall in revenue, market share and market value and saw its market value plummet by over 50 percent in the space of 12 months. Its inability to put adequate emphasis on performance-accelerating behaviour led to its being taken over by a competitor and almost all its management being made redundant.

Balance of behaviour is critically important. Performance-accelerating leadership is not better or more important that performance-sustaining leadership. Both are necessary; nether can survive without the other. The balance varies by industry, and over time. Sometimes rapid change is essential and sometimes stability is important. The most difficult task for any leader, at any level and in any job, is to get the balance right. Individuals and organizations that ignore this do so at their peril.

Chapter summary

Leadership is about getting people from the top to the bottom of an organization to improve their performance. Everyone in an organization has a leadership role to play; the old concept that there are a few leaders and a lot of followers no longer applies. The issue of leadership has been diverted further by two prevalent myths: that leaders are born, not made, and that leadership is a manifestation of personality. Both are tied to the mistaken belief that there is a specific set of traits that all leaders possess – a sort of Holy Grail of leadership. There isn't.

Research shows that there are three underlying ways in which leadership behaviour is demonstrated: a focus on *action* (initiating activities, driving for results, getting things done by dint of personal effort), a focus on *people* (showing concern for people, aiding them in their development, being sensitive to interpersonal needs and relationships) and a focus on *system* (coordination of activities, integration of outputs, strategic thinking and action).

Leadership is about accelerating and sustaining performance. Both are of critical importance, not only to organizations but also to individuals. An analogy might be a Formula One racing car. Acceleration is exceptionally important but the fastest or quickest car does not always win the race. A large percentage of the cars that start don't finish. Having the best qualifying time and the quickest start are not enough; performance has to be sustained for the entire duration of the race. What happens in the pits and what happens to the delicate engineering of the car differentiates between success and failure. Performance-sustaining behaviour is directed towards improving efficiency, getting things done right, ensuring that systems and processes operate optimally, ensuring people have requisite skills, and maintaining quality. It focuses on optimizing results with given resources. Research indicates that upwards of a third of total performance loss can be directly attributed to inadequate levels of performance-sustaining behaviour.

Performance-accelerating leadership is about behaviour that is directed towards improving effectiveness, driving changes and improvements, taking the offensive against competitors, creating vision and direction, generating excitement and commitment, inspiring a winning culture, ensuring that systems and processes operate optimally, and increasing returns. Its focus is to add value by doing things differently and better.

The balance of performance-accelerating and performance-sustaining leadership behaviour is critical for success both for individuals and organizations:

- too much performance-accelerating leadership behaviour and not enough performance-sustaining behaviour results in loss of control and confusion;

- too much performance-sustaining behaviour and not enough performance-accelerating behaviour results in complacency and stagnation.

If leadership is about accelerating and sustaining performance then all those people we talked about at Toyota who continually put forward suggestions for how to maintain and improve quality, how to improve productivity, how to cut costs and generally how to do things better, are demonstrating leadership. Without leadership on the shop floor, management is crippled. It is management's job to encourage and support leadership from everyone, not just from their fellow managers. When that doesn't occur, poor performance always results.

4

What is performance-driven leadership?

The very essence of leadership is that you have to have a vision. It's got to be a vision you articulate clearly and forcefully on every occasion. You can't blow an uncertain trumpet. (Father Theodore Hesburgh, former president of Notre Dame University)

In the previous chapter we talked about leadership in terms of performance-accelerating behaviour and performance-sustaining behaviour and we described in general what we mean by these terms. But what does one actually do to accelerate or sustain performance? What do the specific behaviours look like? In conversations and discussions over a number of years with groups of managers (about 5,000 people in all), the managers identified the specific behaviours that, in their experience, accelerated, sustained or blocked performance. The list of behaviours that resulted from these discussions extends to about 400 specific actions.

When looking at these lists of behaviours that accelerate and sustain performance it becomes clear that there is more than one road to Rome. As we noted in the last chapter, individuals' behaviour at work tends to reflect some combination of focus on action, people or system. Virtually nobody survives and rises in organizations with uni-dimensional behaviour. The reason is that no jobs, staff or managerial, are uni-dimensional. Almost all require elements of direct action, elements of people involvement, and elements of systems and procedures. The required degree of each depends on the job.

Behaviour that is focused on action is characterized by things like taking initiative, setting an example, inspiring and exciting people, setting clear performance targets, monitoring performance against targets, paying attention to detail, and making sure things are completed on time. Behaviour that is focused on people is characterized by things like delegating responsibility and accountability, building teams, creating learning, training and developing, and providing help and support. And behaviour that is focused on system is characterized by things like coordinating activities, integrating outputs and results, long-term planning, making systems work for, rather than against, performance, analysis and assessment. None of these types of behaviour is more or less effective than the others; it depends on the situation. It's a common misperception that to get results your behaviour has to be highly action oriented. That's one of the principal reasons for the failure of entrepreneurs as they move from small operations, which they control personally, to larger enterprises, where they are no longer able to be on top of everything that happens.

Accelerating performance

An action approach to accelerating performance

Example is not the main thing in influencing others, it is the only thing. (Albert Schweitzer)

Most of the examples of business leaders in the media focus on individuals who have a strong action orientation. The more flair they show, the more press coverage they get. Richard Branson is a good example. He projects an image of the daring, decisive, swashbuckling executive whose charisma gets people to follow his leadership. Branson's flair is attractive and essentially benign. He has cast himself as the champion of the little man, taking on the nasty giants. His fight with British Airways was pure David and Goliath. A rather less attractive and more malign caricature of the out-front leader is Albert J. ('Chainsaw Al') Dunlap, former CEO of Sunbeam Corp. Dunlap styled himself as 'Rambo in pinstripes', and laid waste to Sunbeam, driving it, according to *Business Week*, to near bankruptcy.

A quintessential example of an individual who accelerated performance through a strong focus on action was Harold Geneen, the fabled former chairman and chief executive of ITT. He held long meetings with all his top managers – 120 managers in Europe and 130 in the USA – twice a month. He kept his files on the operations of each of the ITT companies in separate briefcases so that he could take them with him to meetings. The company operated some 250 profit centres around the world, and he would question managers in minute detail, having gone over their monthly reports with what his biographer, Alvin Moscow, describes as 'his unerring eye for the erring detail'. There is no doubt about the effectiveness of Geneen's leadership at ITT. Over his 18 years as CEO he and his managers and staff took sales from $756 million to $16.7 billion and doubled profit margins.

But Geneen was a leader, not a celebrity. He never took the sole credit for the success of ITT:

I established high, challenging goals for the company because that's the kind of man I was. I wanted to create an invigorating, challenging, creative atmosphere at ITT. I wanted people to reach for goals they might think were beyond them. I worked as long and hard as any man at ITT and they knew it. But I did set an example, an honest example, which travelled down the ranks and established a standard of performance for the whole company.

Geneen knew who created the results, and like Albert Schweitzer he believed that he could influence these results by setting an example of behaviour for the people who could make a difference.

When the focus of action-oriented behaviour is on accelerating performance the behaviours involve what can be termed 'leading from the front'. They include doing things like setting an example, taking initiative, setting the pace, getting people excited about a vision or a goal, making actions visible and setting clear expectations. To use an analogy, the behaviour is like being a lead dog in a dogsled team. The lead dog is at the front of the team. It sets the pace. It provides the leadership and inspiration for the other dogs. It is not necessarily the biggest or the most dominant, but it is the dog the others trust and will follow. It puts its shoulder to the harness and pulls with all its energy.

For people to be influenced by your behaviour, they have to be able to see it. The lead dog sets the example by being out front. Stelios Haji-Ioannou, founder of the easyGroup of companies, explains how he leads: 'I believe that people will do things if they see their boss doing exactly the same things. Our war meetings are done standing up – there's no better way of signifying urgency.' The underlying message is performance improvement. Role models are important. Performance improvement often requires a spark, an inspiration, to get moving. Behaviour conveys messages far more convincingly than words. There isn't anyone who has lived and worked in a medium or large organization for any length of time who hasn't developed a healthy cynicism about corporate announcements of various kinds. People don't always pay attention to what is said; they watch very closely to see what is done. Anyone can talk the talk, as the saying goes, but what matters is whether they walk the talk.

> **behaviour conveys messages far more convincingly than words**

Some of the specific behaviours that characterize this approach to managing a job are:

- challenging people to raise their goals;
- focusing actions on areas where there is a clear impact;
- setting a vision;
- confronting difficult decisions;
- initiating change;
- creating a sense of enthusiasm and excitement;
- using symbols to dramatize arguments and capture attention;
- leading by example;
- stressing the importance of winning;
- providing a clear direction for people.

Action-oriented behaviour is competitive. There is a striving to be the best, to deliver products or services faster and better, to gain market share, to increase revenues and profits, to beat the competition, to capture their customers and hold them, etc. One of General George

Patton's famous sayings was, 'May God have mercy upon my enemies, because I won't'. This is the victory-or-death approach to competition. The legendary football coach Vince Lombardi is alleged to have phrased it as 'Defeat is worse than death; you have to live with defeat'.

Are these the sorts of behaviours that are necessary for producing top-level results in your job? When you've got to the end of the chapter come back to this and the other lists of behaviours in the chapter and tick off the five or six behaviours you think would help you to improve your performance.

A people approach to accelerating performance

There's no limit to what a man can achieve as long as he doesn't care who gets the credit. (Robert Goizueta, former CEO of Coca-Cola)

An action orientation is by no means the only route to effective leadership. Our research examining the behaviour of several thousand managers shows that while about 45 percent of them exhibit dominant action-oriented behaviour, some 35 percent show dominant people-oriented behaviour, and 20 percent display dominant system-oriented behaviour. When the focus is on a people-oriented approach to accelerating performance, the behaviours include delegating responsibility, creating high-performance teams, giving people recognition for achievement, learning from failure, actively soliciting ideas and suggestions, and recruiting and promoting the best people. The objective of the behaviour is to release the energy and commitment of capable people, to ensure they are challenged in their work, to give them jobs that motivate and excite them, and to give them the freedom to do what they believe is best for the company and its customers. If people are discouraged from taking initiative, they won't. If they aren't allowed to make a decision without having it approved higher up, they will make fewer and fewer decisions. Nothing saps a person's energy and vitality more than being constantly shepherded, cosseted, regulated and nannyed.

People-oriented behaviour aimed at accelerating performance demonstrates one of the key principles of Behaviour Kinetics – ask them, don't tell them. The behaviour focuses on delegating responsibility, building trust, creating strong team relationships, and building commitment to the goals of the unit and the organization. The aim is to produce people who can and will provide leadership and add value. To do that, as Robert Goizueta points out, it's necessary to be able to leave one's ego at home.

Motivation and commitment emanate from the job. They can't be 'injected' into someone. They occur when people are given the opportunity to do what they most want to do, and to do what they feel they are best at. An understanding of this point is the basis for effective people-oriented behaviour. It is an adult approach to getting the best out of people because it recognizes that they are turned on by different things. A good manager will try to find out what those things are for each individual. Niall Fitzgerald describes how he felt when that happened to him: 'I found myself doing something that energized me in a way I'd never been energized before. It was from that moment forward that I thought, hey, this is what I want to do for the rest of my life.'

To accelerate performance, people-oriented leadership behaviour needs to focus on encouraging people to learn and to become the best they can be. While mistakes shouldn't necessarily be encouraged, they should be both expected and accepted. There is no doubt that taking risks can lead to failure as well as success, but taking no risks almost certainly leads to failure. Every mistake is a learning opportunity. Without constant learning and development neither an individual nor an organization can grow.

The behaviour we're talking about here isn't 'soft'. Leo Durocher, legendary baseball player and manager, was famous for saying 'Nice guys finish last'. That's not always true, but managers who put being nice before being effective not only fail themselves but also fail the people whom they lead. People-oriented leadership isn't about being nice or trying to be liked. It's about giving someone the responsibility and authority to do a job – and holding them to that responsibility. It's not for the faint hearted. Delegating responsibility is a contract. If the recipient agrees to take on a job, then they must fulfil their side of the

❝ taking no risks almost certainly leads to failure ❞

bargain – they are accountable for the results. That implies that they will give their very best effort. On the leader's side of the contract, the commitment is to provide necessary support when required – but not to take back the responsibility for the task. Failure is acceptable, given best effort, but people who don't give full and honest effort need to be dealt with summarily. Strong people-oriented leaders make it clear that you can fail if you gave your very best; but if you gave less than full effort, it is a breach of contract which is punishable. Poor performers avoid working for strong people-oriented leaders because they dislike the thought of having to be held accountable for things.

Some of the specific behaviours that characterize this approach to managing a job are:

■ delegating as much responsibility as possible;

■ making sure people live up to their commitments;

■ encouraging risk taking and personal development;

■ actively soliciting ideas and suggestions from people;

■ making sure people get credit for their achievements;

■ recruiting people with high potential to learn and develop;

■ building strong bonds of trust;

■ helping people to learn from failure;

■ encouraging people to identify how they can best add value.

A system approach to accelerating performance

How can you govern a country which has 246 varieties of cheese?
(Charles De Gaulle)

De Gaulle's remark encapsulates one of the great problems faced by management. It's relatively easily to manage vertically; it's getting people across teams, groups, departments or functions to integrate and coordinate what they do that's the difficult part. The third road to accelerating performance is one that is hardly ever written about or commented on, probably because it's not at all glamorous or sexy. It just gets things accomplished smoothly without much fuss or fanfare. It is system-oriented behaviour. Of the managers we have studied, approximately 20 percent exhibited this as a dominant behaviour set.

A system focus on accelerating performance centres on things like creating an effective structure and infrastructure, ensuring that systems, processes and procedures add value, coordinating the activities of various individuals and groups, integrating the output of different teams, departments or divisions, and supporting longer-term, strategic thinking.

Organizations need to achieve a balance between the application of system and procedure and the questioning of it. Rigid and unquestioning compliance leads to rigor mortis; complete disregard ends in implosion. During the time he ran Marks & Spencer, Marcus Sieff claimed that when a problem arose the first place he looked was the system. M&S ran according to a highly articulated system. What made it so successful was that M&S both accepted and encouraged questioning of the system. Questioning had to be based on clear logic and clear values. There was no room at M&S for individual egos. The company began a headlong descent under Richard Greenbury, whose style discouraged questioning of his decisions.

Jorma Ollila, chairman and chief executive of Nokia, says he focuses much of his daily energy on overcoming the stifling bureaucracy that makes large organizations resistant to change. 'People easily slip into their comfort zones and don't ask chilling enough questions of themselves or question the environment they are in.' The mark of effective system-oriented leadership is constant questioning of everything – basic market assumptions, growth assumptions, the way management works, what customers want, etc. But it is only possible to question things if you are not personally attached to them, and managers often fall into the trap of getting their egos and emotions involved.

If structures, systems and procedures are well designed, user-friendly and value adding, then individuals can devote their attention to dealing with the really important issues and not become trapped by mundane and trivial ones. All too often managers spend their days running about stamping out brushfires while the really big problems remain unattended. The goal of strong system-oriented leadership is to create an organization where management by exception is the rule, while systems and processes take care of the day-to-day issues. 'Don't sweat the small stuff' is fine as long as someone or something is dealing with it. 'Small stuff', if left to accumulate, has a nasty tendency of building into big trouble. The role of system-oriented behaviour is to create and implement the processes, procedures and systems that deal efficiently with the small stuff.

Some of the specific behaviours that characterize this approach to managing a job are:

■ coordinating the activities of individuals and groups;

■ integrating the outputs of various different people and teams;

■ seeking best practice and implementing it;

■ building on linkages and interdependencies between jobs;

■ taking a longer-term view of the potential outcomes of decisions and actions;

■ ensuring that systems and processes add value;

■ maintaining a tight focus on the bigger issues facing the business;

■ building networks of contacts;

■ trying to focus on the big picture;

■ making processes and procedures customer driven.

One of the objectives of detailed procedure is to minimize error. Large, high-volume manufacturing operations, or high-volume transactional businesses such as banks, insurance companies and telephone companies, all of which require operations to be performed consistently and to specified standards, require a strong focus on process, procedure, rules and structure.

Sustaining performance

Sustaining performance levels is a critical, if often overlooked, activity in all organizations. The stock market isn't very fond of flat financial performance, but it likes it a great deal more than declining financial performance. Growth stocks get all the publicity but there are a number of 'widows and orphans' investments that provide a steady dividend and that don't fluctuate much in value. These are with companies that manage their revenue streams and costs well, that keep a very close eye on their processes – production, distribution, inventory, collection of accounts, etc. – and sustain a level of consistent performance.

But the need for sustaining performance isn't restricted to companies in steady slow-growth industries; it's essential in all businesses. Simply look at some of the spectacular failures of the past few years and it will become clear that while they were running for growth they failed to pay attention to the essentials of the business. Sustaining performance involves setting clear, measurable and attainable goals; monitoring performance constantly and tracking established targets; planning activity; assessing and analyzing risk; paying attention to detail; ensuring that processes and procedures are implemented; and providing relevant training and development for people.

Quality is all about sustaining performance. Producing one flawless item and lots of flawed ones does not win a quality award; the idea is to produce every item to the same standard and the same specifications. Quality demands high attention to detail; it demands consistent processes and procedures; and it demands constant monitoring to detect any variations in output. These are all performance-sustaining activities. We tend to think of quality more in terms of product than of service, but to be successful, companies in service industries also need to focus on quality. Any definition of quality is largely subjective. The Six Sigma definition is 'reduction of variation around the mean'. In other words quality equals consistency, given that the mean level is satis-factory. The quality mean is quite different for McDonald's and Gordon Ramsey, but consistency is critical for both of them and consistency comes from concentration on performance-sustaining behaviours.

" quality is all about sustaining performance "

An action approach to sustaining performance

If you're not part of the steamroller, you're part of the road.
(Rich Frank)

An action approach is at the heart of effective performance management. It involves doing things like clarifying objectives, getting agreement and commitment to them, consistently tracking performance against them, picking up on where things are not progressing smoothly, and dealing with the missing details. It is designed to keep operations on track and take projects and tasks through to completion. Measurement is a key component in an action-focused approach to sustaining performance. To maintain consistency and to ensure that things get done on schedule and to specification, there have to be unambiguous measurements.

This is hands-on management with close concentration on what is going on, close attention to all the necessary detail, and involvement – in terms of being constantly informed of progress – at every stage of the process. Action-focused performance-sustaining behaviour concentrates on the implementation of strategy. It is execution. It deals with the tangible and concrete and puts order into activity. This is a highly focused and disciplined approach to work. Successful commercial organizations all understand the importance of this type of behaviour.

Some of the specific behaviours that characterize this approach to managing a job are:

- responding to problems and situations rapidly;
- completing tasks on schedule;
- setting clear, measurable and attainable objectives;
- doing things right first time;
- paying close attention to detail;
- monitoring performance against targets;
- clarifying performance expectations;
- setting and focusing on priorities;

- rewarding output rather than input;
- applying strict quality standards.

A people approach to sustaining performance

Anyone who has never made a mistake has never tried anything new.
(Albert Einstein)

The focus of a people-oriented approach to sustaining performance is to create a culture of help and support, to provide people with appropriate training and development, and to create a feeling of loyalty and family at work. It's not an easy task and it tends not to be done well in most large companies. Our research shows it to be the least used style of behaviour in both large commercial and non-profit organizations, and a survey conducted by the Hay Group in 2005 confirms our findings. It showed that only 40 percent of employees thought their companies did a good job of retaining high-quality workers. Almost 60 percent thought that performance evaluations were unfair, and 42 percent rated the job training with which they were provided as poor. They generally felt they had few opportunities for advancement, and – even more damning – they claimed that even if there were opportunities, they didn't know what they needed to do to take advantage of them. As to creating a feeling of loyalty and family at work, only half of the front-line staff surveyed believed their company took a genuine interest in their welfare.

The finger of blame for these types of findings is often pointed at human resources departments, but while they are far from blameless, the responsibility for making performance assessment meaningful and helpful, for retaining high-quality people, for clarifying the behaviour and performance needed for advancement, for creating opportunities for advancement, and for creating a feeling of family and loyalty to the organization lies firmly with line managers. If they don't want to create a culture of help, support, challenge, development and opportunity for people, they have to suffer the results of not doing so.

The behaviours that characterize a people-focused approach to sustaining performance all reflect a sense of honesty and a genuine desire to help people do their jobs well, to help them develop their skills and abilities, and to advance their careers. The 'family' model dominates much of the behaviour of people-focused performance-sustaining behaviour. Like good family members, these leaders take care of their own, look out for them, help them, support them through difficulties, encourage them, are loyal to them, respect them and give them self-respect. They sustain performance because they sustain people, and performance can't happen without people.

The view of Frederick Taylor and Henry Ford of people as simply another cog in the production machine still holds sway in many managers' minds. It was the way General Motors managed its people, as opposed to the way Toyota manages its people, and the relative performance of the two companies should be enough to drive a spike through the heart of Taylorism and its derivatives.

Some of the specific behaviours that characterize a people-oriented approach to sustaining performance are:

- treating people with respect and dignity;
- making sure people have the necessary skills to do their jobs;
- creating an atmosphere of trust and support;
- giving people a sense of belonging;
- encouraging contributions from everyone;
- accepting mistakes and learning from them;
- soliciting ideas and suggestions from people;
- giving recognition for good performance;
- rewarding initiative;
- rewarding ideas and suggestions.

The major difference between the behaviour of people-focused leaders in roles that require them to accelerate performance rather than sustain performance is how they approach the issue of motivation. In terms of Maslow's hierarchy of needs, accelerating performance requires a focus on the higher level needs – esteem from others and self-actualization. The behaviour centres on getting people to take responsibility for themselves, to challenge themselves, to take risks and stretch themselves, and to grow and develop. Performance-sustaining behaviour, on the other hand, tends to focus on Maslow's lower level needs – physical well-being, belonging and self-esteem. It concentrates on trying to make sure working conditions are good, that jobs are secure, that people feel a part of something (team, group, company, etc.), and that they have interesting and worthwhile jobs that make them feel positive about themselves.

Once again, organizations need a balance of both these types of people-oriented leadership behaviour. Often the lower levels of the motivational hierarchy are taken for granted, but experience clearly shows examples where neglect of these elements has negative effects higher up the chain. For example, when people feel insecure (downsizing, mergers, acquisitions, restructuring), their concerns revert to more basic needs like security which, if not attended to, result in things going awry. Performance is not sustained, quality declines, productivity falls, and normal functions and tasks fall by the wayside. At the same time, when people are not recognized for what they do, when they don't have any sense of the importance of what they do, and when they don't feel they are able to achieve anything, efficiency and effort both decline.

A system approach to sustaining performance

The successful person makes a habit of doing what the failing person doesn't like to do. (Thomas Edison)

The emphasis of system-focused performance-sustaining behaviour is a consistency of process, predictability and stability. It attempts to ensure people follow accepted practice rather than making ad hoc decisions. It makes sure that systems and processes are implemented and applied, that precedent is weighed and considered, and that rationality is given priority over emotion.

This approach is unfortunately often equated with bureaucracy; a bureaucrat being defined as 'an official who is rigidly devoted to the details of administrative procedure'. The word 'rigidly' says it all. But that's not what system-focused sustaining behaviour is about. Compliance with process and procedure is most definitely at the heart of it, but it is important to recognize that process and procedure are what ensure consistency and predictability. Done effectively they produce stability; done poorly they produce rigidity. Even though they move, a ship, an aeroplane, a car or a human body all need to have stability. They need to go through defined sets of motions. Rigidity implies no movement at all, and rigidity tends to make ships rust and sink, aeroplanes to fall out of the sky, cars to disintegrate and human beings to expire.

> **process and procedure are what ensure consistency and predictability**

System-focused performance-sustaining behaviour is about maintaining the framework around or within which an organization operates. It makes the elements of an organization's infrastructure work – the communication network, production processes, financial systems and controls, definition of jobs and roles, compensation systems, purchasing procedures, the distribution systems, etc.

Some of the specific behaviours that characterize a system-oriented approach to sustaining performance are:

- keeping information up to date;
- ensuring that processes and procedures are followed;
- making sure similar situations are dealt with consistently;
- carefully assessing the consequences of variations to procedure;
- detailed planning;
- breaking complex problems down into manageable pieces;
- assessing risk;
- eliminating system blockages.

Chapter summary

Performance results from the application of a combination of sustaining and accelerating leadership behaviour. Both of these forms of leadership behaviour can be manifested in different ways. The principal ways in which they are demonstrated are through a focus on action, people or system, or some combination of these. Action-oriented behaviour is characterized by things like taking initiative, setting an example, inspiring and exciting people, setting clear performance targets, monitoring performance against targets, paying attention to detail, and making sure things are completed on time. People-oriented behaviour is characterized by things like delegating responsibility and accountability, building teams, creating learning, training and developing, and providing help and support. And system-oriented behaviour is characterized by things like coordinating activities, integrating outputs and results, long-term planning, making systems work for rather than against performance, analysis and assessment. None of these types of behaviour is more or less effective than the others; it depends on the situation.

Action, people and system-orientation behaviours differ depending on whether the objective is to accelerate performance or sustain it. Action-oriented accelerating behaviour centres on taking initiative, setting the example and creating enthusiasm and energy. When the focus is on sustaining performance the behaviour involves doing things like clarifying objectives, getting agreement and commitment to them, tracking performance against them, and maintaining attention to details.

People-oriented accelerating behaviour focuses on delegating responsibility, building trust, creating strong team relationships, and building commitment to the goals of the unit and the organization. When the focus is on sustaining performance the behaviour centres on creating a culture of help, support, loyalty and a feeling of 'family' at work, and making sure people are treated with dignity.

System-oriented accelerating behaviour focuses on things like creating an effective structure and infrastructure, ensuring that systems, processes and procedures add value, coordinating the activities of various individuals and groups, integrating the output of different teams, departments or divisions, and supporting longer-term, strategic thinking. When the focus is on sustaining performance the behaviour centres on ensuring and maintaining consistency of process, predictability, rationality and stability. It's about making the framework of the organization work – the communication network, production processes, financial systems and controls, definition of jobs and roles, compensation systems, purchasing procedures, the distribution systems, etc.

5

What is performance-blocking behaviour?

A man who has committed a mistake and doesn't correct it is committing another mistake. (Confucius)

While we know that certain actions accelerate performance and that other types of action sustain performance, there is a third set of behaviours, which have negative consequences and undermine performance. These are behaviours that obstruct change, subvert vision, and hinder the achievement of goals and objectives. We call them performance-blocking behaviours.

A great deal of the energy, effort and drive of people is lost to organizations through blocking behaviour. The behaviour is, unfortunately, a fact of organizational life. We see it both in others and ourselves every day at work, and we take it for granted as part of the human condition. Because everybody displays some negative behaviour, we tend to do nothing about it and view it as just another obstacle to be overcome. But overcoming obstacles requires energy, and that energy would be much better applied to doing positive, value-adding things.

Over his 70 or so years of observing organizations, Peter Drucker has reached the conclusion that 'There are an enormous number of managers who have retired on the job'. This is a rather devastating indictment of management's failure to come to terms with the problem of blocking behaviour. We are all aware of people in our own organizations who have retired on the job. These are people who have been affected and infected by blocking behaviour. They have learned that it is not a good idea to take a risk, to show initiative, to state a position on an issue, or to stand by a decision. They have learned to be submissive, to be evasive, to become as invisible as possible, to sniff the wind and move with it, to keep a low profile and to play at being a 'team player'.

But why have so many people, managers and staff, 'retired on the job'? The answer, in the vast preponderance of cases, is that they have been on the receiving end of blocking behaviour and as a consequence they have adopted coping mechanisms that cause them to engage in reciprocal negative behaviours. A 1999 study by Roffey Park Management Institute showed that 57 percent of the 353 managers surveyed were considering leaving their jobs because of poor management and lack of recognition. 'Poor management' is a euphemism that covers the full range of blocking behaviours. They are behaviours that leave people feeling stranded and at risk, which threaten them, which place unwarranted pressures on them, or which demean them.

Why do people engage in performance-blocking behaviour?

Performance-blocking behaviour is caused by external pressures and influences. It is not a personality issue. As a rule people don't want to fritter away their time and energy. They generally don't want to be counter-productive or disruptive. They would prefer to be part of something positive, something which gives them personal reinforcement, boosts their self-esteem and self-concept, and makes them feel proud of their own, and their associates', achievements. But they are driven to blocking behaviours when they are actively prevented from this. A great deal of performance-blocking behaviour results from the frustration of being robbed of self-worth.

" performance-blocking behaviour is not a personal issue "

When people find themselves in situations over which they have little or no control, when they feel they are at the whim of forces beyond their grasp, when they feel threatened and intimidated, when they have been placed in jobs beyond their capabilities and are not getting support and backup, when they are not able to get decisions from their bosses and others, and when they are made to feel isolated and at risk, they react by engaging in performance-blocking behaviours. Virtually all performance-blocking behaviour is a reaction to external factors and forces. It is not driven by personality; it is driven by poor management, poor systems, poor structure and poor interpersonal relationships.

Performance-blocking behaviour at work

Here are a few examples of the poisonous effects of blocking behaviour. They will no doubt remind you of situations in your own experience.

A medium sized insurance company had been losing market share for three years. As well as having a declining customer base, its margins and profits were falling. A new chief executive was brought in to turn things around. He duly assessed the situation, laid it out clearly to the entire management group, put forward a plan of action, and solicited the suggestions and ideas of his executive. There was generally stated agreement. But one of the senior managers did not agree with the steps being suggested, and without making his objections known to the CEO or the team, made it clear to his people that they were not to do anything without first consulting him.

When approached by members of his team, this senior manager refused to take any action or make any decisions. The people in his department were on the one hand being bombarded by pressures for change and, on the other, handcuffed by their inability to get anything done. It took the CEO some time to grasp what was going on, and more time trying to get the manager to support the changes. The result: the manager was finally removed, but widespread frustration and disillusionment remained in the department, and blocking behaviour was rife throughout it. Many of the department's managers had 'retired on the job', to use Drucker's phrase. The loss to the firm was not just one individual whose behaviour had soured, but a large number of managers who had been infected by his actions. Responsibility avoidance in one individual is itself destructive, but the poison it spreads to others whom it annoys, frustrates and emasculates is far greater.

Performance-blocking behaviour is not, however, limited to responsibility avoidance. It manifests itself in a variety of ways. As an animal species, humans react to threat, challenge, frustration, anxiety or uncertainty in one of three fundamental ways: fight, flight or submission. Depending on their early life experience some people attack when threatened, some run away, some acquiesce. Make no mistake, however: the underlying cause of the behaviour is a reaction to a perceived threat, not merely a manifestation of personality. The reaction exhibits itself as *behaviour* and as such can be controlled. Nobody *has* to do anything. Behaviour is voluntary.

One of the regions in a large multinational technology firm was suffering from abnormally high rates of turnover among senior country managers. Competitors were making major inroads in the market, and targets being set at corporate level were not being met. There is nothing particularly unusual about intense competitive pressure, or about short-term setbacks in various markets, but the problems seemed to persist and a salient characteristic of the situation was a 25 percent annual turnover in senior managers. A diagnosis of the circumstances indicated large amounts of blocking behaviour among managers in the region. At a meeting of all the Country General Managers (CGMs) within the region, their senior marketing and finance managers, and the Regional Chief Executive, the reason became clear.

The meeting's agenda was to set and agree volume and profit targets for each country unit. After a day of presentations from several CGMs, in which their forecasts for the coming year were all in line with the overall regional targets, and in which the previous year's below-target results were rationalized in a variety of ways, the regional CEO blew up. He rounded on them for having said and done the same thing for the past two years – rationalizing past performance, doing nothing to correct the problems, falsifying current-year performance, and presenting knowingly unrealistic volume and profit targets in the full knowledge that they would not be able to reach them. He accused them of withholding information, and of a dereliction of duty and responsibility that merited them all losing their jobs. He left in a rage.

The room sat in stunned silence. But after a moment or two it erupted with utterances of frustration, grievance, dissatisfaction, and both rebellion and resignation. The discussion never regained a positive note. The strangest aspect of the behaviour was that rather than the general managers and their marketing and finance directors supporting one another, the CGMs, all of whom had been rolling over for the regional CEO all day, now turned on their own people and accused them of withholding information, lying, etc. – a complete mirror of the earlier performance!

This type of aggressive-defensive behaviour is rarely ignored by those on the receiving end, and seldom forgiven. Recipients of the behaviour either strike back in some fashion or take pains to get out of the way and stay there. In this instance the regional CEO's intimidating behaviour stifled initiative and motivation in his CGMs and they passed on their sense of futility to their teams. Many became retired on the job. And many simply retired *from* the job, as the attrition rate of senior managers demonstrated.

Blocking behaviours result from frustration, uncertainty, anxiety, threat, belittlement, and lack of power or control. But they also become the *cause* of blocking behaviours in others by passing on these things. Here is an example of another type of blocking behaviour: conflict avoidance.

The marketing director in a division of a large FMCG company spread the poison of negative behaviour and energy wastage in a subtle way. An outwardly charming and sociable man, his major skill was to sense political wind shifts. Over a career in the company spanning more than two decades he was renowned as never having put a foot wrong. But also as never having taken any risks or initiative. He charmed his superiors, bamboozled some of his colleagues, and frustrated the rest of the people working for and around him. He was a master of conflict avoidance, never disagreeing with anyone if possible. What drove others to distraction was the fact that they could never be sure of what he would do, since he agreed with whomever he had talked to last. Managers would leave his office sure they had his support for something, only to find he had backtracked and now appeared to be supporting another course of action. His boss was blind to his behaviour and supported him. Many of his subordinates went into virtual retirement on the job because they realized that any effort to drive change and take initiative was fruitless. More than a few good people left. The negative effects of his behaviour were only cut off when the company was taken over and he lost his job.

The behaviour that squanders energy, undermines motivation, destroys initiative, and turns productive people into at best, cynical, jaundiced, weak, unenthusiastic and pessimistic individuals, or at worst into antagonistic, destructive, aggressive bullies is in almost all cases caused by factors external to the individual. Behaviour is learned. It is created by the environment, and in the case of the behaviour of people at work, is caused in large part by an organization's management and culture.

Blocking behaviour is infectious

The really unfortunate aspect of blocking behaviour is not simply that a few individuals in an organization may be wasting time and energy doing non-productive or counter-productive things, it's the widespread negative effect that their behaviour has on others. Blocking behaviour is highly infectious. When individuals flare up at others and, wittingly or unwittingly, demean or intimidate them, there are two possible consequences: people get mad and back away from involvement, or people get mad and get even. When managers avoid responsibility for making decisions they create an atmosphere of anxiety and uncertainty among their subordinates and peers that makes them reluctant to make decisions, take initiative or take risks. In this type of environment they tend to become cynical and demotivated. The same sort of thing occurs when individuals go to some lengths to avoid conflict, constantly change their position on issues, or refuse to express an opinion. This creates massive frustration among the people with whom they work, and tends to turn them into responsibility and risk-avoiders.

Blocking behaviour begets more blocking behaviour. Blocking behaviour is the way individuals vent their frustrations, anxieties and anger, but while the venting relieves some of the pressure on the person doing it, the people at the receiving end find it rather less gratifying.

ff blocking behaviour begets more blocking behaviour ""

Being at the receiving end of vented frustrations is a bit like being on the pavement when a car speeds through a large puddle in front of you. In spite of the fact that you are a completely innocent party you get drenched by a wave of dirty water and the car speeds off oblivious to it all. The individual venting their frustration is often blissfully unaware of the effect on others. They just enjoying the relief of letting it all out, and having done that, like the speeding car, move on without the slightest idea of the damage caused.

Blocking behaviour and continuous performance improvement

The CPI process addresses blocking behaviour right from the start. The first two steps of the process – answering the questions 'What are you doing now?' and 'What should you be doing differently to improve your performance?' – are designed to cut blocking behaviour off at the pass. An AT ('ask them') approach is absolutely essential. It's one thing to accept the positive things that you are doing and quite another to accept that you may also be doing things that have negative consequences, but this acceptance is critical. A basic principle of Behaviour Kinetics is that the start point for any behaviour change is understanding and accepting what you are doing now.

As we mentioned earlier, human beings all possess a screening system that attempts to filter out feedback that is threatening to the self-concept. It generally doesn't filter out all negative feedback but it does a pretty good job on a great deal of it. However, the less threatening the feedback, the greater its chance of getting past the screen and being accepted. The thing that takes much of the threat out of feedback about blocking behaviour is that the behaviour is the product of forces external to the individual. Because you exhibit some blocking behaviour it doesn't mean you're a bad person or that you have a dysfunctional personality. What you are doing is a normal reaction to various stresses and strains generally not of your own making. Blocking behaviour is normal. Everyone indulges in it at some time in one form or the other. But it's controllable. You don't have to do it. It can be moderated; it can be stopped; it can be re-channelled into positive, value-adding behaviour.

The causes of blocking behaviour may be external, but the cures are internal. You are the person who has to do something about it. You should be able to work out what it is that makes you exhibit blocking behaviour and try to deal with the cause. Getting rid of the cause is a great deal more effective than treating the symptom. Exhibiting blocking behaviour is understandable; continuing it after you've been made aware of it is unforgivable.

The first step in the process is to identify your specific blocking behaviours – the specific ways you duck conflict, avoid responsibility or vent your frustration. Examine your own behaviour. Here are some specific blocking behaviours that people commonly exhibit at work. Do you do any of the following things? Do you:

- Criticize people in public?
- Vent your frustration and anger openly?
- Make it difficult for people to challenge your opinions or decisions?
- Alter your stated opinion rather than get into an argument?
- Bend the rules to keep the peace?
- Avoid giving people negative feedback?
- Avoid stating where you stand in arguments?
- Guard information closely?
- Make it difficult for people to contact you?
- Avoid making decisions on controversial issues?

If the answer to any of these questions is yes, then the next thing is to identify when you do these things and what is causing the behaviour. There is a reason why you do these things. What is that reason? None of these are positive behaviours. They all get in the way of accelerating or sustaining performance. Some are the result of feeling threatened, some are the result of being frustrated, some are due to anxiety or uncertainty, some are due to feeling demeaned, ignored, undervalued or overlooked. There are a variety of different causes but they tend to boil down to a sense of loss of control and a loss of self-esteem. Very normal. We all have these feelings. The issue is what we do about them.

Try to recognize when you're becoming frustrated, recognize when you feel threatened or uncertain, and recognize when you feel resentful at being snubbed or ignored by someone. You need to be in tune with your underlying feelings and then you need to observe how you react to them. Are you able to keep your feelings and emotions in check and not let them influence your behaviour? If you are, then you're a special type of person, because most people find it exceedingly difficult to do that with any consistency.

Once you recognize how you react to various things, you can begin to think about how to deal with them. Can you influence the causes of your frustration, anxiety, etc. in any way? Can you moderate your reaction to these things? For example, if you get irritable and somewhat aggressive when you are pressured to meet deadlines, is there something you can do to overcome this? Could you work out how to plan a little better or get started on things earlier? Or could you set firm goals and priorities and resist being pulled away from them and being drawn into other people's crises?

If you want to decrease your performance-blocking behaviours, the best way to is to get feedback from people who work closely with you about what you do, when you do it and what effect it has on others. Or seek feedback by using a behavioural diagnostic questionnaire. If you want to change your behaviour and improve your performance, then dedicate some time and effort to the process.

You can't change your behaviour until you know exactly what you're doing now. And you won't change your behaviour unless you acknowledge and accept what you're doing. Acceptance and under-standing of a situation is a prerequisite to being able to decide what to do about it. The steps are simple: acknowledge the behaviour; determine the cause; deal with the cause; if you can't get rid of the cause then change the way you react to it. You won't lose weight until you acknowledge you are overweight. Once you acknowledge the fact, the next step is to look for and find what's made you/is making you overweight – the causes. And the third step, if you really want to reduce your weight (and remember, people only change when they see the light or feel the heat) is to deal with the causes. If you can't control the cause because it's something like having to attend compulsory business lunches and it would cause offence if you didn't eat whatever is presented (which sounds like a somewhat extraordinary circumstance, but let's go along with the assumption) then change the behaviour you can control, and take more exercise.

> **you can't change your behaviour until you know exactly what you're doing now**

The same process applies to getting other people to reduce or stop their performance-blocking behaviours. First, you need to get them to recognize and accept what they are doing. Then you need to help them identify and examine the causes of their behaviour. Only when you've achieved these two things will they be able to move to the third step and decide whether to change their behaviour or not.

If the cause of your behaviour is beyond your control, then you need to deal with your reaction to it. There is an old prayer, attributed originally to St Francis of Assisi but more recently claimed by Reinhold Niebuhr: 'God grant me the serenity to accept the things I cannot change, the courage to change the things I can, and the wisdom to know the difference'. Sometimes you can change the things that are frustrating, unsettling or annoying you, and sometimes you can't. If you can't change something, then you need to try to change the way you think about it and the way you respond to it. Organizational life isn't smooth. There are constant distractions, constant conflicting demands, constant stumbling blocks to progress. These things tend to evoke an emotional response and blocking behaviours are all manifestations of emotion. They indicate that you've been 'got at'. The trick, and we're not saying it's easy, is to try not to let these frustrations get to you, but to keep your emotions under control and to view the situation rationally and calmly.

However, having said that, it's also important to be able to recognize when things are completely outside your control and when, no matter how hard you try to moderate your response to them, they are taking a toll on you. Stress is directly related to performance-blocking behaviour. If you read the literature on stress and look at its symptoms – frustration, anxiety, uncertainty, feelings of diminished self-worth, hostility, defensiveness, etc. – and then look at blocking behaviour and its causes you will find a one-to-one match. If you find yourself in a job that is stressing you a great deal and there is no way you can deal with the factors causing the stress, you might consider changing your job. High levels of stress over a period of time have rather severe physical consequences.

Focusing behaviour

The amount of time, effort and commitment that anyone can devote to a job is, by definition, limited. There are only so many hours in a day or week and there are limits to physical and mental energy, even though these may be stretched. Life and work are more fruitful, more rewarding and lead to greater achievement if the energy we have available is focused toward positive ends – change, improvement, excitement, challenge, quality, excellence, results, development – rather than being wasted dodging responsibility, shying away from risk, avoiding initiative, avoiding argument or controversy, or pressuring and intimidating people in a futile attempt to get them to do things against their will.

Energy and effort by themselves are not enough for success. Achieving excellence also requires clear focus. Concentrating effort on clearly defined targets increases the chances of success geometrically. Highly focused people who waste little time and energy outside the target zone of their objectives and ambitions get the results they want. Individuals whose energy is dispersed over unclear goals get fewer clear wins. People with clear goals accomplish far more in a shorter period of time than people without them could ever imagine.

Perhaps the most highly visible example of focused mental and physical energy is professional sport. Extremely high levels of focus and concentration are the norm for top-level sports people. At the top level in any sport all the participants have the physical attributes and the skills and abilities of champions. What separates the consistent winners from the rest is the ability to focus all their energy and will on the specific behaviours that lead to a clearly defined goal and to stop doing the things that get in the way of achieving that goal.

Of course, it's not easy to maintain a clear focus on getting things done effectively all the time. Everyone experiences 'bad days' – days when it is difficult to concentrate on the task at hand, when disturbing things are happening at home, when one feels ill, when private worries supersede the work immediately to hand, when organizational politics and interpersonal problems in the workplace divert attention, when pressures build, when unexpected failures occur, etc. All these diversions deflect and re-channel energy. They often result in energy wastage and blocking behaviour, all of which is understandable but all of which is also, with a little effort and focus, controllable.

In any kind of organizational context, blocking behaviours can never be defined as 'good' or 'appropriate'. They are behaviours that are non-productive at best and counter-productive at worst. They can be highly negative and value destroying. They are actions of which none of us are proud, although quite often we do them without recognizing what the outcomes are or how others perceive them. Blocking behaviours often become particularly evident in cases of mergers, takeovers, or downsizing – situations with which an increasing number of people are becoming familiar. In these situations individuals spend inordinate amounts of time scratching about for information as to what is likely to happen to them and their jobs. Their attention is diverted from doing their job to worrying about their future, their security, their career, their options, etc. The anxieties, uncertainty and perceived threat of this type of situation are highly distracting. The percentage of time and effort devoted to organizational and job issues decreases significantly.

Blocking behaviour is almost always correlated with a feeling of loss of, or lack of, power and control. Behaviours that leave people feeling demeaned or denigrated, feeling thwarted, feeling unvalued or feeling scapegoated bring forth reactions that sharply divert energy and attention from productive ends. Takeovers, for all but the most senior or specialized among the 'overtaken', are an extreme example of loss of power and control. Nothing in the situation is certain; few of the criteria for survival and success are clear; there are innumerable pressures, both open and hidden in the system; there are always winners and always losers; and there are great frustrations around not knowing what to do or what not to do.

Fear, uncertainty and frustration are powerful negative motivators. A research study (by Ryan and Oestreich) of 260 managers in the USA found that more than 44 percent of conflict avoidance behaviours and responsibility avoidance behaviours – i.e. blocking behaviours – resulted from fear of repercussion. And another 17 percent were due to frustration – 'nothing will change as a result of anything I do'. A survey of 500 workers in the UK in 2003 revealed that 77 percent of them felt their jobs were at risk over the next year.

These are worrying statistics. While part of this feeling of insecurity (which almost always translates itself into some form of energy-wasting,

> **ff fear, uncertainty and frustration are powerful negative motivators** 🗩🗩

blocking behaviour) may be due to the uncertainties of change, the majority is due to negative management. If your boss won't be honest about plans for change, won't show clear support for you, won't make a decision, won't lay out or agree clear objectives for you, won't stand by an agreement, intimidates you or embarrasses you in public, how 'secure' do you think you're going to feel? And if you don't feel overly secure, how proactive are you going to be? How much initiative are you likely to take? How much change are you likely to drive? How much vision and excitement are you likely to bring to your job?

And what about you personally? How do you treat the people who work with and for you? Are you honest with them about plans for change? Do you show clear support for them? Do you make your decisions visible to everyone? Do you agree clearly defined, measurable objectives with people? Do you stand by what you've agreed to, and not backtrack or change your position? Do you intimidate people, or embarrass them in public? If you do these negative things, then expect negative consequences. Here's a bit of advice from one of the most successful businessmen who ever lived, Sam Walton, the founder of Wal-Mart, the world's largest corporation:

If you manage through fear, your people will be nervous around you after a while. They won't approach you with a problem, so the problem gets worse. They will be afraid to be creative or express a new idea. They don't feel they can take a chance because they won't want to risk your disapproval. When this happens the people suffer and the business suffers too.

Chapter summary

Blocking behaviours obstruct change, subvert vision and hinder the achievement of goals and objectives. We all see people doing these things and we do them ourselves, but it is generally not something that is talked about or focused on. More often than not it gets brushed under the carpet. However, its results can be devastating for performance. One result is what Peter Drucker describes as individuals who are 'retired on the job'.

Performance-blocking behaviour is caused by external pressures and influences. It is not a personality issue. It results from frustration, uncertainty, anxiety, threat, belittlement, and lack of power or control. The really unfortunate aspect of blocking behaviour is not simply that a few individuals in an organization may be wasting time and energy doing non-productive or counter-productive things, it's the widespread negative effect that their behaviour has on others. Blocking behaviour is highly contagious.

Blocking behaviour is almost always correlated with a feeling of loss of, or lack of, power and control. Behaviours that leave people feeling demeaned or denigrated, feeling thwarted, feeling unvalued, or feeling scapegoated bring forth reactions that sharply divert energy and attention from productive ends. Fear, uncertainty and frustration are powerful negative motivators.

If you want to decrease your performance-blocking behaviours, the best way is to get feedback from people who work closely with you about what you do, when you do it and what effect it has on others. Or seek feedback by using a behavioural diagnostic questionnaire. If you want to change your behaviour and improve your performance, then dedicate some time and effort to the process. You can't change your behaviour until you know exactly what you're doing now. And you won't change your behaviour unless you acknowledge and accept what you're doing.

The causes of blocking behaviour may be external, but the cures are internal. You are the person who has to do something about it. You should be able to work out what it is that makes you exhibit blocking behaviour and try to deal with the cause. Getting rid of the cause is a great deal more effective than treating the symptom. Exhibiting blocking behaviour is understandable; continuing it after you've been made aware of it is unforgivable.

6

What does performance-blocking behaviour look like?

Bad habits are eliminated not by others, but by ourselves.
(Vince Lombardi)

Performance-blocking behaviour is a reaction to a threat of one kind or another. In a work setting it centres on a threat to your self-esteem, your competence, knowledge and ability, your worth and value, your control over career and destiny, your job security, and your ability to exert power and influence. It generally involves a loss of some kind or, more starkly, a feeling of being robbed or stripped of something. Our reaction to threat manifests itself in three ways: fight, flight or submission. While personality exerts little influence over performance-accelerating and performance-sustaining behaviours, it does play a role in determining the type of blocking behaviour an individual exhibits when they are subjected to threat. Depending on their personality, some people react to threat with aggressive behaviour (fight), some react by distancing themselves from the situation (flight), and some react by giving in and acquiescing to the pressure (submission).

Defensive-aggressive behaviour

Defensive-aggressive behaviour occurs principally as a reaction to a perceived attack on self-esteem. Self-esteem is boosted by success and degraded by failure. But failure is a question of degree. It depends on how important the task is. When the outcome of something is perceived to have a bearing on your reputation, standing, authority, credibility or power base, the potential for falling into the trap of defensive behaviour is increased quite dramatically. Look behind defensive-aggressive behaviour and you'll often find a fear of failure.

While managers who lose their temper and tear a strip off subordinates may feel better for 'having got it off their chest', the people around them are unlikely to be sympathetic and understanding. Rather, they find this type of behaviour upsetting, embarrassing, belittling and insulting. They see the manager as immature and undisciplined. The behaviour may massage the manager's emotions fleetingly, but it inflicts longer-term bruising on others, and causes a large amount of energy loss among people on the receiving end. Vernon Walters, former US ambassador to the UN, puts it quite nicely: 'If you humiliate people publicly, they may support you publicly, but they will hate you privately'.

The consequences of significant defensive-aggressive behaviour are long lasting and can inflict serious damage. 'Chainsaw' Al Dunlap, the man who, as CEO of Sunbeam almost drove the company into the ground, was an extreme example of this type of behaviour. *Business Week* described his behaviour in these terms: 'In Dunlap's presence, knees trembled and stomachs churned. Underlings feared the torrential harangue that Dunlap could unleash at any moment. At his worst, he became viciously profane, even violent.'

There is no excuse for this sort of behaviour. It is the product of an overweening ego and unchallenged bullying. Fortunately not too many people quite this distasteful rise to senior positions. As Eric Hoffer, the great twentieth-century American social philosopher observed, 'Rudeness is the weak man's imitation of strength'.

Defensive-aggressive behaviour is not always manifested in an overt 'throw the toys out of the pram' mode. People are often good at communicating annoyance or frustration through subtle non-verbal means. You do not have to shout and carry on to communicate threat or anger. Tone of voice, posture and gesture get the message across very clearly. Despite the lack of vivid fireworks, the result is the same: the recipients feel bruised and resentful.

Defensive-aggressive behaviour is often displaced aggression. In other words, the individual is annoyed at, or frustrated by, something or someone that has nothing to do with the present set of circumstances, but

> **❝ projecting your frustration on to others doesn't solve anything ❞**

they vent their anger and frustration on a poor unfortunate who happens to be in the wrong place at the wrong time. When you get a roasting from your spouse or companion for a trivial matter, you know there's something else that's bothering them. When you go over the top because of some small issue, you would be well advised to ask yourself what the real problem is. Projecting your frustration on to others doesn't solve anything. It just makes it many times worse because you may create another enemy in the process. We all do these things from time to time. The point is to recognize when you're doing it – and stop yourself.

Defensive-aggressive behaviour can be a reaction to pressure for increased performance from above and inadequate performance from below. This situation is not at all uncommon in large organizations. An individual is given performance targets but achievement of the targets depends on the performance of others. However, when the 'others' are not delivering, the individual becomes the meat in the sandwich and feels increasingly powerless. Frustration and anxiety begin to exhibit themselves in displays of annoyance, in increasing pressure on the people who aren't delivering, in tightening control over them, in policing their activities, or in punishing them.

People who exhibit defensive-aggressive behaviour are sometimes individuals who have very high personal standards of performance. They become disappointed when others fail to match these standards. Their disappointment can manifest itself in anger and annoyance. There is nothing wrong with having high standards. However, there is a lot wrong with demeaning others who don't match up to them. Having high personal standards is not an excuse for arrogant, dominant and insensitive behaviour that demeans people. This behaviour is also the height of hypocrisy. Individuals who exhibit this type of behaviour are in reality nothing more than bullies. The website BullyOnline claims that the work rate and effectiveness of someone subjected to bullying is reduced by 50 percent.

Defensive-aggressive behaviour also comes from falling into the trap of thinking that everything depends on you and that you have to take personal responsibility for whatever happens. In situations where one feels fully responsible for a wide range of things and the fear of failure looms, the defensive-aggressive reaction is to tighten control, check every detail, supervise more closely, and do everything yourself, hence taking responsibility away from others. The results are predictable: people become less committed, less involved and less interested, and performance decreases.

Defensive-aggressive behaviour also commonly occurs when requests or instructions have been given hastily and poorly and misunderstandings have occurred. This is a communication problem, not a performance problem. But very often people are reluctant to admit to not communicating their wishes clearly and instead pass the blame on to others. The anger, the added pressure, and the resultant recriminations create a vicious cycle where trust levels erode and performance gets worse.

Virtually all behaviour is learned. Much like spoiled children, when individuals persist in defensive-aggressive behaviour they have learned that they can get away with behaving badly. People who exhibit dominant defensive-aggressive behaviour only persist because no one stands up to them and tells them what they are doing, how it is perceived and what the results are.

Do you resort to defensive-aggressive behaviour when you're frustrated or feel under some sort of attack? Look at the following list and check off whether you do any of these things. Do you:

- Show when you're annoyed with people?
- Pressure people?
- Lose your temper when you get frustrated?
- Keep tight control of what people do and how they do it?
- Make it difficult to challenge your opinions or decisions?
- Openly criticize people's failures?

What is making you behave this way? Is the cause something you can influence or control? All these behaviours, while they may make you feel better at the time because they allow you to relieve some of the pressure you feel on yourself, make other people feel worse.

Take a minute here to look back at the list, and put yourself in the situation of the person at the receiving end of these behaviours. As you go through them, one at a time, write down how you feel when each of these things happens to you.

If you get four or five of your friends and colleagues to go through the same exercise you'll find that they write down much the same set of words that you wrote down. We all react emotionally to these behaviours and our reactions are remarkably similar to other people's. Nobody likes being treated this way and when we are at the receiving end of these types of behaviours we tend to react negatively. We see it, quite justifiably, as being unfair and if possible we'd like to even the balance. There are a million and one ways in which people can do that and none of them are designed to accelerate or sustain performance; they all block it in some way or other.

Conflict-avoidance behaviour

The principal cause of conflict-avoidance behaviour is the perception of conflict situations as win–lose, with the associated expectation of there being a high probability of ending up as the loser. When viewed in that manner, engaging conflict conjures up a picture of significant amounts of energy drainage, all in a losing cause. Life's too short for that. Nobody needs to pour energy and effort into a bottomless pit.

So this type of behaviour focuses on avoiding controversy, avoiding risk, avoiding challenging others' opinions, avoiding giving negative feedback to people, avoiding giving constructive criticism, and generally attempting to indicate agreement to points or decisions made by others, whether agreement is real or not. It can be extremely frustrating for people who work with individuals that behave in this way. They can never get a real decision; they can never get a genuine opinion; they can never get any honest feedback. They simply don't know where they stand, and it makes them apprehensive, disheartened and often angry – all of which causes further wasted energy. Problems require solutions and decisions have to be made. Papering over arguments and the clash of opinion, or making the wrong decision because of a fear of upsetting people, simply creates a greater problem in the long run.

While conflict avoidance does not, at first glance, appear to be particularly performance blocking in itself because it does not seem to get in the way of others' plans, actions or decisions, it is a generator of huge amounts of frustration, uncertainty and anxiety. Conflict-avoidance behaviour is a carrier of the blocking-behaviour virus. Its perpetrator avoids becoming involved in any arguments, discussions or potentially controversial decisions and continues happily on their way, while the people with whom they should be interacting become increasingly frustrated and annoyed and end up engaging in performance-blocking behaviour themselves.

Conflict-avoidance behaviour thrives in highly bureaucratic organizations where slavishly following system and procedure offers protection from any accusation of error, and individualism and risk taking result in strong negative consequences. The culture of many organizations is such that there is no reward for success, but there are draconian penalties for failure. Both success and failure are defined as being outside the bounds of the rules and procedures of the system and imply a violation of them. Many government departments and agencies are characterized by this type of culture, and the old television programme *Yes Minister* caricatured it wonderfully.

> **conflict-avoidance behaviour thrives in highly bureaucratic organizations**

Conflict-avoidance behaviour also tends to occur when people are new in a job, or when they feel that changes, which have a direct effect on them, are beyond their control. They make the assumption that if one is 'nice' to others – i.e. doesn't argue with them – they will be nice back. In life in general being polite, considerate, concerned and caring for others usually results in people reciprocating these behaviours. However, sycophantic behaviour generally elicits dominant behaviour in return.

Examples of conflict-avoidance behaviour can be seen in many everyday situations – in something as commonplace as customers' behaviour in a restaurant. A group of people who are dining together find the food/service/table or something else (which could be dealt with by the restaurant staff) is not adequate. The waiter/waitress/manager comes to the table and asks if everything is satisfactory, but rather than tell them about the problem, the party agrees that all is fine. Then privately they fume and complain and vow never to return. A great deal of energy goes into the grumbling and grousing. The issue can dominate conversation for some time. But not only does it waste energy on something that could easily be fixed, the restaurant never gets the feedback about what it has done wrong and it loses custom because it can't make the necessary changes.

Individuals' negative behaviour sometimes results from pushing positive behaviour beyond its limits. For example, highly action-oriented people sometimes continue pushing when there is no need and this results in annoyance, frustration and resentment on both their part and the part of the people who are being pushed. The same applies to conflict-avoidance behaviour. Individuals who are genuinely concerned about people, making sure that they are treated fairly and properly and given support and encouragement, sometimes don't know when to stop being helpful and considerate and supportive. There are times when people don't *want* help. Sometimes they just want to be able to get on with things on their own. They want to be treated as mature individuals who can make their own decisions, take their own actions and live with the consequences. Individuals who are constantly shepherding and mothering people often simply annoy them.

The more insidious effect of conflict-avoidance behaviour is that it tends to lower standards of performance. Because conflict avoiders are unwilling to deal with performance problems in case it results in argument and discord, some individuals are seen to get away with poor performance, half-hearted effort, or purposeful negative behaviour. This makes other people demotivated and they in turn lower their own standards. As a Wells Fargo executive put it: 'The only way to deliver to the people who are achieving is not to burden them with the people who are not achieving'. This view is supported by the research Jim Collins did when writing *Good to Great*. He observed that 'Strong performers are intrinsically motivated by performance and when they see their efforts impeded by carrying extra weight, they eventually become frustrated'.

Conflict-avoidance behaviour has a long fuse and a slow burn and it spreads a poison that is difficult to eradicate.

Do you engage in conflict-avoidance behaviour at times? Do you do any of the following sorts of things? Do you:

- Go to some lengths to avoid disagreement?
- Avoid stating where you stand in arguments?
- Avoid confronting people about poor performance?
- Give the appearance of agreement to avoid argument?
- Avoid giving negative feedback to people?
- Sit on the fence on disputed issues?

If the answer is yes, then take a minute again to think about why. And think about how you would/do react when you are the object of these behaviours. Do you feel comfortable? Or do you feel frustrated? If you're interacting with someone who never lets you know where they stand in arguments, who will never disagree with anything you say, who won't say anything about blatantly poor performance, and whose position on issues is never clear, doesn't that make you feel somewhat unsettled? We all prefer certainty to uncertainty and conflict-avoidance behaviour creates high levels of uncertainty for its recipients. Their reactions are seldom focused on accelerating or sustaining performance.

Responsibility-avoidance behaviour

The principal cause of responsibility-avoidance behaviour is fear of castigation for making a mistake. Henry Ford is quoted as saying, 'Failure is the opportunity to begin again, more intelligently', but fear of failure is a powerful motivator of negative behaviour. It is not simply the idea of failure itself that drives the behaviour; it is fear of what others will think, say or do when one fails that is at the heart of the matter. Organizations that punish mistakes tend to have a disproportionate percentage of people who exhibit responsibility-avoidance behaviour.

This behaviour is the reciprocal of aggressive-defensive behaviour. Subordinates of high aggressive-defensive managers show a high degree of responsibility avoidance and conflict avoidance. If all you get is a harangue when you do something that the boss doesn't like then you (a) stay clear of the boss as much as possible and (b) say you agree with whatever the boss says and does, whether you do or not.

Responsibility-avoidance behaviour manifests itself in withdrawal, reduced involvement in issues or arguments, and apparent disinterest. Experienced practitioners of the behaviour learn to lower their visibility, sometimes to the point of becoming almost invisible. It is chameleon behaviour, blending in with the background and staying clear of potential risk. The phrase 'keeping one's head below the parapet' sums up the behaviour rather nicely. However, it's important to recognize that problems won't go away on their own. Ostrich-like behaviour doesn't solve problems; it just removes them from sight temporarily.

> **ostrich-like behaviour doesn't solve problems; it just removes them from sight temporarily**

Responsibility-avoidance behaviour is the reaction to stress, threat, uncertainty and frustration that removes an individual from the source of the discomfort. However, while individuals who turn their back on difficult situations may allay some of their own anxieties and frustrations, they pass them on to others. If a colleague or a boss avoids responsibility, someone else has to take it. The phrase 'passing the buck' implies that someone 'catches the buck'. In some organizations empowerment, which in principle should be positive and motivating, turns out to be a do-it-yourself hangman's kit. A manager in a large international electronics firm described how she viewed empowerment in her company: 'You get given this responsibility, get no resources or support, and have the feet cut out from under you if you fail to deliver'. As you might imagine, taking responsibility for anything in that company became rather like a game of pass the exploding parcel.

Another cause of responsibility-avoidance behaviour is responsibility overload. You are doing a job and you get asked to take on some additional piece of work – and then another and another and another.

When your phone rings it's often someone at the other end with a problem – and it's not a problem they want to solve, it's one they want you to solve. But you're already overloaded with work. So what do you do? Not answer the phone? Shut yourself in your office? Leave a message that you're 'in a meeting'? Get out of the office? These are all responsibility-avoidance behaviours, albeit often for a good reason. The problem of overload is real. The solution is simple, yet for some people it is difficult to implement. It involves knowing when to say no – and saying it. A common cause of responsibility-avoidance behaviour is an inability or unwillingness to set clear priorities and to stick to them. Being overloaded with work is almost always related to not being clear about priorities.

Responsibility-avoidance behaviour is sometimes little more than the spoilt-child syndrome. When things don't go their way the reaction of adult-size spoilt children is to walk away in a snit. 'If you don't want to play the game my way, I'm taking my ball and going home.' Some individuals have never grown up, and it's because no one has challenged them about their childish behaviour. The only way to deal with this behaviour is to ignore it. Sulking isn't much fun if nobody comes to coax you back to the game.

However, most responsibility-avoidance behaviour is generally the product of plain bad management. When an organization's culture is overly controlling, when success is overlooked but initiative is punished, when new ideas and risk taking are discouraged, when the focus of systems is on setting up procedures to stop people doing things rather than on creating an atmosphere of dynamism, enterprise and inventiveness, a 'battered manager' syndrome may appear.

We know about battered children and battered spouses and see some of the results of their horrible experiences. And we know that the battering can be just as much psychological as physical. Of course, the battering of people in organizations is not physical; that's assault. That leaves marks and it's punishable by law. The battering in organizations is much more subtle. It doesn't leave physical bruises or cuts, but it does cause psychological scarring and it does result in stress and illness. People get brow-beaten, bullied, coerced, intimidated, belittled, berated, criticized, shamed, embarrassed, reprimanded for honest mistakes and humiliated for taking risks. But they learn quickly, and they learn not to stand out from the crowd, not to take risks and not to take initiative – in short, they learn to become invisible. And they tend to have long memories. 'Once bitten, twice shy' is something managers should think about when they deal badly with colleagues and subordinates.

Widespread responsibility-avoidance behaviour in an organization is a reflection of over-bureaucratized management, or management that holds people in low regard, or management that is indecisive and changeable, or management that is censuring of mistakes – in other words, just plain bad management. It is critically important for managers to remember that people do not behave this way naturally. They learn the behaviour from negative experiences. If you have responsibility avoiders working for you, ask yourself how they got that way.

Do you engage in responsibility avoidance behaviour at times? Do you do any of the following sorts of things? Do you:

▨ Try to avoid being held solely responsible for things?

▨ Avoid firm time commitments for getting things done?

▨ Keep a low profile on issues?

▨ Distance yourself from others' failures?

▨ Avoid sharing information with others?

▨ Cut yourself off from people at times?

If the answer is yes, then again take a minute to think about why. And think about how you would/do react when someone with whom you work – a close colleague, your boss, or someone who works for you – behaves like this. Do you 'catch the buck' that they let pass, or do you stand back and let it slip by you? Does their behaviour frustrate you? Do you feel you can trust them to do something that you need to have done? Have you thought about why they act this way? Is there anything you can do to help them change the way they behave?

The cost of performance-blocking behaviour

There is a massive cost associated with blocking behaviour. A wage or salary is paid on the assumption that an individual's time, ability and effort will be directed towards organizational goals and activities. If we pay for a 40-hour week we would like to receive 40 hours of organizationally oriented effort in return. Everyone knows that's not going to happen and they build a certain amount of slack into the equation. But the underlying assumption is still that they will receive a significant percentage of the 40 hours in focused effort. But how much is 'a significant percentage'? Ninety percent? Seventy percent? Forty percent? Forty percent seems too low and 90 percent appears a bit optimistic. But is the assumption acceptable that one can never get 90 percent or more of an individual's effort and energy applied to the job? What level of non-performance is acceptable? Why do we have to accept non-performance at all? Or worse, why do we accept negative performance? Is there something we can do to deal with it? Can we re-channel the wasted, negative energy that goes into performance-blocking behaviour and transform it into energy that is directed towards positive performance-enhancing behaviour?

In a large organization, the application of 100 percent of everyone's energy and behaviour to organizational goals is unlikely. The mind wanders from time to time, concentration wavers, and other agendas take precedence. We see highly disciplined professional athletes, whose livelihood is directly related to their achievements, lose concentration, and the required time span of their activity is generally a great deal shorter than a manager's work week or even a work day. Wasted energy seems to be a fact of life. Some degree of negative, blocking behaviour seems to be distributed throughout organizations. The issue is how to minimize it.

Blocking behaviour causes two problems. At a personal level it causes stress and can lead to depression. At an interpersonal level it causes stress in others that can also trigger a cycle of depression. When people interact with someone exhibiting blocking behaviours, the individuals on the receiving end become demotivated, less focused, less energetic and often more angry, more antagonistic and more resentful. It's important to remember that blocking behaviour is highly contagious.

An example of blocking-behaviour paralysis

The tax collection department of a local London borough council that was experiencing low levels of performance and high levels of absenteeism conducted a diagnosis of the behaviour of its managers and staff. Prior to the diagnosis, management was of the view that what was needed was a recruitment programme that would bring in 'better' staff. Their opinion was that it was neither the environment nor the nature of the work, but the individuals doing the job that was driving the poor performance. If the 'right' individuals were in place, they argued, performance would improve.

The department head planned to have the 70 or so people in his group engage the first stage of the process by completing a diagnostic questionnaire. Immediately the low level of trust was flagged when one entire section refused to participate on the basis that it believed the process was simply what it termed 'a management trick'. Even more disturbing was the fact that several of the top performers in the rest of the department also refused to enter the process. The words they used to articulate their rejection spoke volumes: 'I've done this sort of thing before, and I can't see what it could possibly tell me that I don't know already. The problems are with management and what will this change in them? I don't see how this will possibly change the way we are treated.'

The department's managers exhibited a high level of defensive-aggressive behaviour but were seemingly unaware of what they were doing. One manager said she felt that she was open with people and would frankly discuss all issues with her team. However, during a team meeting it transpired that this frankness amounted to venting her anger openly about people above her and people who worked for her. The culture of the organization, as measured by the behaviour of its managers, punished errors and mistakes (but did not engage the issue of months of backlogged work – i.e. performance) while at the same time overlooking any special achievements. Positive reinforcement and reward were notably absent, while criticism and reprimand were ubiquitous.

It will come as no surprise, therefore, that the behaviour of the staff showed high levels of responsibility avoidance. Management's view was that this behaviour was simply a reflection of the poor quality of staff. They argued that staff had to be told precisely what to do and be tightly controlled and monitored. They were also of the opinion that staff did not feel any responsibility for doing a good job and that it was therefore a waste of time and energy to assume they would work well without close supervision.

Following the steps of the continuous performance improvement process, the individuals taking part in the diagnosis were first asked (using a behavioural diagnostic questionnaire) to identify what they were currently doing to manage their jobs, and then asked the second key question: 'What do you think you should be doing differently to improve your performance?' Management were shocked to find that in fact their staff 'universally wanted to be given responsibility, wanted to organize their work better, wanted to coordinate their work with that of their colleagues, wanted to produce quality output, and believed that the application of process and procedure was important'.

As we've shown, blocking behaviour at the top creates blocking behaviour at the next level, and so on. If left untreated it can eventually infect an entire organization. Individuals working in the borough council wanted to take responsibility and wanted to do a good job; management's behaviour was stopping them from doing so and causing them to react to the frustrations they felt from being treated as being worthless. In the commercial world poor performance triggers action to deal with the problem, but in non-commercial enterprises – unless there are clear performance criteria and these are reinforced by reward and sanction – the virus can create a near fatal paralysis.

Blocking behaviour and stress

Not surprisingly blocking behaviour is linked to stress. The UK Health and Safety Executive defines stress this way: 'Stress is the reaction people have to excessive pressures or other types of demands placed upon them. It arises when they worry that they can't cope.' (A somewhat more graphic definition is 'Stress is when you wake up screaming and you realize that you haven't fallen asleep yet'.) There is a strong correlation between the amount of blocking behaviour exhibited by an individual and the level of stress that they are experiencing. Blocking behaviour is a symptom of something else. It is a reaction to the factors that cause stress. But symptoms can be painful. The symptom of stomach ulcers is excruciating stomach pain. Until relatively recently, the treatment focused purely on the symptom and not the cause. Once the cause was discovered – a bacterial infection – treatment could focus on it, with the result that stomach ulcers are largely a thing of the past.

If you can find what is causing an individual to exhibit performance-blocking behaviour then you are well on the way to helping the individual reduce the level of stress they are undergoing. Sustained high levels of stress, characterized by such things as chronic anxiety, sustained sadness or pessimism, persistent tension, deep-rooted suspiciousness or massive frustration, have hugely debilitating effects. For starters they double the risk of heart disease, asthma and arthritis.

Performance-blocking behaviour is a behavioural manifestation of stress. Stress and stress-related illness represent a massive cost to organizations. Stress is increasingly becoming a significant issue in the lives of millions of individuals and is also costly, both in terms of personal health and well-being and in terms of productivity. In the UK, according to the Health and Safety Commission, 33 million work days were lost to stress in 2001, compared to 18 million in 1995. A major employee assistance provider in the USA reported a 23 percent rise in stress counselling from client companies in 2003.

The research study of 260 individuals mentioned in the previous chapter found incidences of managers at all levels using blocking behaviours – threat and intimidation, withholding of information, creation of frustration, creation of uncertainty and anxiety, unwarranted pressure, lack of recognition for effort and achievement, failure to give people responsibility, and actions that reduced people's self-esteem. The killer finding, however, was that these behaviours caused the people on the receiving end to engage in reciprocal blocking behaviour. Some 70 percent of the 260 interviewees admitted to engaging in negative behaviours themselves as a result of being managed negatively.

Depressingly, one of the researchers' observations was: 'We are confident that the greatest percentage of intimidating behaviours are committed unconsciously by managers who have no idea of how their behaviour is affecting others'. Here is the nub of the problem. We don't confront the problem. The researcher may well be correct; much of the behaviour may be unwitting, but that is precisely the issue. Until it is brought to the attention of people it will continue and they will be excused because they did these things 'unconsciously'. People have to be made aware of how their behaviour affects others. 'Having no idea of how the behaviour is affecting others' is not an admissible excuse, any more than ignorance of the law excuses criminal acts.

❝ people have to be made aware of how their behaviour affects others ❞

Without clear identification and measurement of the specific blocking behaviours in which people are engaging, the situation can never resolve itself. The behaviours will continue and the poison will spread, propagating more blocking behaviour and energy wastage, and causing mental and physical debilitation to people on the receiving end. Revenues, profits, service quality and productivity will remain suboptimal. Performance-blocking behaviour can, and must, be identified. Its perpetrators must be made to realize what they are doing. People don't do these things because they want to or because they have warped personalities. They do them because they are driven to do them. Deal with the causes and cure the problem.

Chapter summary

Our reaction to threat manifests itself in three ways: fight, flight or submission. While personality exerts little influence over performance-accelerating and performance-sustaining behaviours, it does play a role in determining the type of blocking behaviour an individual exhibits when they are subjected to threat. Depending on their personality, some people react to threat with aggressive behaviour (fight), some react by distancing themselves from the situation (flight), and some react by giving in and acquiescing to the pressure (submission).

Defensive-aggressive behaviour occurs principally as a reaction to a perceived attack on self-esteem. The consequences of significant defensive-aggressive behaviour are long lasting and can inflict serious damage. Defensive-aggressive behaviour is often displaced aggression. It can also be a reaction to pressure for increased performance from above and inadequate performance from below, or the result of having high standards to which others cannot rise. However, no matter what the cause of the frustration, displays of anger and annoyance only subtract from performance. Much like spoiled children, when individuals persist in defensive-aggressive behaviour they have learned that they can get away with behaving badly. People who exhibit dominant defensive-aggressive behaviour only persist because no one stands up to them and tells them what they are doing, how it is perceived and what the results are.

The principal cause of conflict-avoidance behaviour is the perception of conflict situations as win–lose, with the associated expectation of there being a high probability of ending up as the loser. This type of behaviour focuses on avoiding controversy, avoiding risk, avoiding challenging others' opinions, avoiding giving negative feedback to people, avoiding giving constructive criticism, and generally attempting to indicate agreement to points or decisions made by others, whether agreement is real or not. It can be extremely frustrating for people who work with individuals that behave this way. They can never get a real decision; they can never get a genuine opinion; they can never get any honest feedback. They simply don't know where they stand, and it makes them apprehensive, disheartened and often angry – all of which causes further wasted energy.

The principal cause of responsibility-avoidance behaviour is fear of being punished for making a mistake. Organizations that punish mistakes tend to have a disproportionate percentage of people who exhibit responsibility-avoidance behaviour. Responsibility-avoidance behaviour is the reaction to stress, threat, uncertainty and frustration that removes an individual from the source of the discomfort. It manifests itself in withdrawal, reduced involvement in issues or arguments, and apparent disinterest. Experienced practitioners of the behaviour learn to lower their visibility, sometimes to the point of becoming almost invisible. It is chameleon behaviour, blending in with the background and staying clear of potential risk. The phrase 'keeping one's head below the parapet' sums up the behaviour rather nicely. The behaviour is generally a reflection of management that holds people in low regard, or management that is indecisive and changeable, or management that is censuring of mistakes, or over-bureaucratized management – in other words, just plain bad management.

The cost of blocking behaviour is huge. The energy expended on blocking behaviour is energy that could be focused on accelerating or sustaining performance. Because of its basic contagious nature, blocking behaviour creates waves of further blocking behaviour that spread throughout the organization like the ripples from a rock dropped in a pond. It is clearly linked to things like stress, which alone accounts for about 33 million lost working days a year in the UK.

7

What makes people whistle on the way to work?

We know nothing about motivation. All we can do is write books about it. (Peter Drucker)

Any discussion about continuous performance improvement must address the issue of motivation. An underlying principle of Behaviour Kinetics is that people change because they want to, not because someone else wants them to. The question, of course, is why do they want to?

There are many incorrect assumptions about motivation. For example that motivation is a personality trait; you either have it or you don't. Or that money is what really motivates people. Or that people are motivated by a stirring message. Of course it depends on who delivers the stirring message. Winston Churchill's famous opening line, delivered in his first speech to the House of Commons as prime minister, 'I have nothing to offer but blood, toil, tears and sweat', roused a nation, but when Bart Simpson delivered the same line to a war council in his tree house his audience walked away.

Motivation is simply the willingness to exert effort to attain goals. The higher your motivation to achieve a goal, the higher the level of effort you are willing to exert. Motivation is not a personality trait. Everyone is motivated to do various things. Understanding individuals' motivations is difficult because what appears to be the same action can be motivated by quite different goals. We eat because: we are hungry; we are nervous or stressed; we like the taste of something; we want to gain/lose weight; we wish to address a vitamin balance issue; we were told by our doctor we had to; etc. Regardless of the basic motivation for eating, which is to sustain life, the reasons people do it, when they do it, how much they do it, and so on, are endless.

When we say someone is not motivated, what we often mean is that they are not motivated to do what *we* think they should do. A sports coach wants a player to practise more, concentrate harder and go through various drills. When the player doesn't, the player is said not to be motivated. Absolutely right. They are not motivated to do what the coach wants because what the coach wants so badly is not wanted that badly by the player. So the old joke line has the coach asking, 'What's the problem; is it intelligence or is it apathy?' To which the player answers, 'I don't know and I don't care'.

Logic has relatively little to do with motivation. More often than not motivation to do things is based on emotion rather than logic. The flaw in the idea that a logical argument will persuade people to do things (i.e. motivate them to action) is based on the underlying assumption that what *we* see as logical is the same as what others see as logical, and that they have the same thought processes that we do.

Does personal charisma motivate people to do things? The answer is sometimes yes and sometimes no, but generally only when they want to do these things anyway. If charisma was an essential prerequisite for motivational leadership then there must be some mysterious force that has made so many boring and bland politicians, military leaders and business people able to motivate people to perform extraordinary acts. According to Peter Drucker, Harry Truman, one of the USA's most effective presidents, had no charisma at all. The reason we all remember charismatic people like Winston Churchill or General Patton or Walt Disney is because they were different from the thousands of other politicians or business people of their time. But they represent a tiny fraction of successful political, military or business leaders.

And as for external incentives like salary, bonuses, benefits (or even 'negative incentives' like threats), a mountain of research evidence points to the fact that they have little or no impact on effort or perfor-mance. If you are being paid £50,000 to do a job, will you put in ten times the effort for £500,000? If you are already working 40 hours a week, how can you work 400 hours? You may give more effort if . . . and there are also a whole lot of reasons why you may not.

A sticker on the cover of the January 2003 issue of the *Harvard Business Review* proclaimed it to be a 'special issue on motivation'. How could anyone resist? The motivation to understand motivation is compelling. Perhaps the most interesting thing about the journal was that of its eight major articles, four had been written more than 25 years earlier. It appears that despite the fact that the basic research on motivation has been available for almost three decades, we don't want to listen to the message.

Films and books seem to tell us that motivation in management is something that people do to other people. Various individuals are seen as 'good motivators'. That's a TT approach. But motivation is much more of an inner state rather than something that one person does to another. People are motivated to do things when *they* want to do them, and when they want to they'll do them without prompting. Motivation can come and go. There are days when we feel highly motivated and days when we feel like staying in bed. Motivation stems from what we are, what we want to be, what we need, and what makes us feel good about what we do. It therefore depends on the individual and the goal. So if you want to find out what motivates someone, a TT approach is shooting in the dark. You have to find a way to ask them that elicits a valid answer.

Getting the answer wrong

The problem with motivation starts because we all think we understand what motivates other people – and we don't! Chip Heath, from Stanford University, has conducted some very interesting research that shows quite clearly that managers are very bad at judging what motivates employees. In every one of his studies he finds what he calls 'extrinsic incentives bias', which, in everyday language, means a bias towards thinking that other people are motivated mostly by external rewards

like pay, bonuses, benefits, etc., and not much by things like responsibility, recognition and achievement. In all his studies he finds that

> **managers are very bad at judging what motivates employees**

managers think that the people who work with and for them (and whom they claim to know and understand well) value pay and other extrinsic rewards much more than they actually do – and more than the managers themselves do. Why is it that people can describe their own motivators as things like challenge, having the opportunity to achieve things or recognition, but not believe that other people are motivated the same way?

People in all walks of life fall victim to this error about motivation. When 500 young people hoping to enter law school were asked what their basic motivation for pursuing a legal career was, two-thirds of them said it was because they found it intellectually interesting. However, when they were asked what they thought the motivation of *others* who were making the same choice was, more than 60 percent said it was principally for the money. Only 12 percent of the students ascribed their own motives to others. It is a very strange phenomenon, but we can't seem to recognize that other people may be motivated in a similar fashion to ourselves.

A survey undertaken annually by the University of Chicago asks a random sample of adults across the USA to rank the importance of pay, security, free time, chance for advancement, and opportunity to do work that gives them a feeling of accomplishment. Work that provides a sense of accomplishment ranks first, and pay third. But what is most interesting is that when the same people are asked to rank what motivates others, 75 percent say pay is first and around 65 percent say that they don't believe other people are motivated by taking on additional responsibility (i.e. doing something that gives them a feeling of accomplishment) unless they get extra pay for it.

When Lou Gerstner was president of Amex International, he drew a distinction between what he called a 'ticket of entry' and a 'competitive advantage'. External rewards such as pay, bonuses, benefits, etc. are tickets of entry, but they don't create competitive advantage in people.

Pay and good external rewards are adequate to convince employees to spend time with the company, but they are never enough to convince them to give all they have to achieve the company's goals. Competitive advantage is achieved through things like challenge, recognition for achievement, giving people a feeling of importance, and enabling them to make a meaningful contribution. Compensation and benefits only compensate for the sacrifice of time; they don't engender initiative and going the extra mile.

Motivation and movement

One of the best pieces of work on motivation was published in 1959 by Frederick Herzberg. His research was extensive and has been replicated many times. It may come as no surprise that academics have found a variety of ways to criticize Herzberg's research. They cite beautifully trivial arguments about things like research methodology. The fact is that his findings reflect reality and stand up to the test time and time again.

Herzberg talks about the difference between motivation and movement. He says that when extrinsic rewards are used it is the manager who is motivated and the subordinate who moves. He describes the process as like training a dog to do things by giving it biscuits. When it rolls over it gets a biscuit and when it doesn't roll over it either gets nothing or it gets a punishment. The dog trainer/manager is the one who's motivated and who therefore feels responsible for the dog's/individual's behaviour. The dog/individual just moves when there is a short-term reward on offer, and doesn't move when there is no specific reward.

Herzberg describes being motivated as like having an internal generator that gets one to do things without external rewards. Being *moved* – doing things as a result of extrinsic rewards – implies having internal batteries that need to be charged up each time you're requested to do something. Charging the batteries keeps responsibility firmly in the hands of the manager. Internal generators give it to the individual. The observation of the leadership expert Ken Blanchard springs to mind: 'As a manager the important thing is not what happens when you *are* there, but what happens when you are *not* there'. What happens when the battery charger is not at the office?

Motivation and behaviour

There is an obvious connection between motivation and behaviour. From an organizational point of view the issue is not whether people are motivated to act but whether they are motivated to act in specific ways that add value to the organization. So how can motivation be harnessed and channelled in such a way as to improve organizational performance? The principles of Behaviour Kinetics provide the answer.

> **❝ what you do a lot of is most likely to be what you find rewarding ❞**

The first step is to find out from the individual what they are currently doing. Thorndike's law of effect says that we do things when they are rewarding and pleasurable, and that we stop doing, or avoid doing, things when they are unrewarding, disagreeable or unpleasant. Therefore, what you do a lot of is most likely to be what you find rewarding – i.e. it's likely to be something that is meeting your motivational needs.

For once Peter Drucker may be wrong. We *do* know something about motivation. What we know is that motivation comes from the job, from the task, from the role. You can try to get people excited with external things like prizes or games or speeches if you wish, but we know that these things often don't work very well, and that even when they do the effects wear off quickly. Present people with the opportunity to do something that they like doing and you're much more likely to hit the motivational nail on the head.

It might be helpful if you knew why an individual liked doing something, but you don't have to. All you have to know is that when you give Janet a chance to exercise her creativity she does it well, and when you give her a job that is tedious and detailed she doesn't do it well. Janet is motivated by creativity, not by predictability and repetition. On the other hand, when you give Peter a job that is complex and requires careful attention to detail, he always delivers the goods. Watch what people like doing, and what they therefore tend to be good at, and try to give them these sorts of jobs. That's the first major step to getting people motivated.

Expectation and behaviour

Expectations play an interesting role in the behaviour of people in organizations. They can be viewed from two different perspectives: expectations that individuals have of themselves and expectations that others have of them. Both affect behaviour.

One of the reasonably well-researched theories of motivation is expectancy theory. Expectancy theory states that individuals tend to act in a certain way based on the expectation that a given act will be followed by a given outcome with a given level of attractiveness. It seems rather obvious that most things are done with an expectation, conscious or unconscious, of an outcome. This is Thorndike's law taken one step further. Just as what gets measured gets done, what gets rewarded gets done again. Your expectation of reward – whether through raised self-esteem, praise from others, or feelings of pleasure from having completed an action and experienced its outcome – has a clear and obvious influence on your actions.

There is a great deal of research that supports the fact that what managers expect of people – and the way the managers project those expectations – has a major effect on behaviour and performance. One of the earliest and most compelling studies was conducted in the Metropolitan Life Insurance Company in the USA. The manager of a district office at MetLife decided to conduct an experiment with his agents and assistant managers. He assigned the best six agents in the office to the best assistant manager in the office, six average agents to an average assistant manager, and the rest of the agents (low producers) to his least productive assistant manager. Then – and here comes the expectation part – he gave the top-rated group (less than one-third of all the agents in the office) a target of achieving a sales volume equal to 65 percent of what the entire office had achieved the previous year.

The results were astonishing. Overall agency performance improved by 40 percent. The following year a fourth assistant manager was appointed in the office and the agents allocated to each of the assistant managers were once again selected on the basis of best agents with best assistant managers, average agents with average assistant managers, etc. Agency performance increased another 30 percent.

While the performance of the group on whom the highest expectations were placed continued to rise, the performance of the group deemed to be the least effective declined, and attrition increased. Low expectations produced low performance, and low performance produced low satisfaction and low feelings of self-esteem. It should not have been any surprise that the bottom-rung performers, having been constantly compared unfavourably with the top performers, left the company. Who needs to be consistently told they are failures?

It is currently popular to talk about A, B and C performers and about the need to weed out C performers. But there is little information on how to *transform* B and C performers into As. High-profile managers like Jack Welsh trumpeted the success of constantly weeding out the poorest performers at General Electrics, and Chainsaw Al Dunlap turned the process into an art form at Scott Paper. What absolute nonsense! Crassness and brutality do not bring about long-term high performance. The performance that the chainsawers claimed resulted from their managerial brilliance was nothing more than the general effect of a raging bull market and unprecedented sustained economic expansion.

What actually made the clumsy experiment at Metropolitan Life succeed, in terms of overall performance for the entire office, was that the assistant manager who had been given the agents rated as merely average refused to accept that they were any less capable than the agents in the top group. She made a point of telling them (and she did it in a way that showed she believed it) that she felt they had even greater potential than the agents in the top group and that she thought they could outperform them. Not surprisingly, this middle group increased its productivity by a greater percentage each year than the top group. How fortunate for the manager who began the experiment. Had it not been for this quite remarkable woman, whose self-confidence and spirit were not to be quashed by the arbitrary opinion of higher management, the same fate would have befallen the 'average' group of agents as occurred with the lowest-rated performers.

The motivational dynamics of expectations involve things like self-esteem, feelings of achievement and other psychic rewards. This has several implications. First, the source of the expectation needs to be credible. In the MetLife case, the assistant manager who felt her agents were every bit as good, and had just as much potential, as the so-called super-agents, was perceived as a credible source. Her agents believed her and respected her. Second, the source of the expectation needs to be someone, or some group, whose praise, esteem and recognition are valued. And third, the individual has to believe that there is a realistic chance of succeeding at meeting the expectation.

> **"the individual has to believe that there is a realistic chance of succeeding"**

It's not just what someone says about their expectations, but what they do to back it up. Because people respond so sensitively to expectations, their ability to read whether those who express the expectations genuinely believe they can be met is highly acute. What people fail to understand, or don't wish to accept, is that we tend to be much better at communicating low expectations to people than we are at communicating high expectations. The general manager in the Metropolitan Life office had real problems in accepting that he had communicated his low expectations very clearly to the agents whom he had labelled as the poorest group. But the agents got the message loud and clear and it sounded to them like 'We really don't want you around here'. When one of them left and the manager told him he was sorry to see him leave, the agent replied 'No you're not; you're glad'.

If expectations are perceived as unreasonable, individuals will not be motivated to try to meet them. This is illustrated by the hundreds upon hundreds of instances where sales or production targets have been set unrealistically high, with the result that people have simply stopped trying to meet them. This happened at Sunbeam when the aforementioned Al Dunlap set targets that were patently unreasonable. To meet his revenue targets, Sunbeam would have had to increase sales five times faster than its competitors. To meet his target of increasing operating margins to 20 percent in a year, Sunbeam would have had to increase its profitability (2.5 percent at the time) by a factor of 12. Expectations like that aren't motivating. All they do is spread a feeling of hopelessness.

Motivation and Behaviour Kinetics

Let's start with the premise that an individual's frequently demonstrated behaviour is a reflection of their motivation – i.e. what you do a lot of is what makes you feel good about yourself. Accepting that as a premise means that we can deal with things that are observable, measurable and changeable – behaviours – rather than things which tend to be more intangible like attitude and personality. It also means that we can apply the basics of Behaviour Kinetics to the understanding and application of motivation.

The first question that Behaviour Kinetics raises is what individuals are doing currently, and the second is what they think they should be doing to improve their performance. We know that the vast majority of behaviour in the workplace is related to the demands of the work itself, so while you may be doing a number of things to manage your current job effectively it does not necessarily mean that these are things that you find particularly gratifying or motivating. As the lyric to the Rolling Stones song goes, 'You can't always get what you want', and everyone recognizes that. But there's no reason why you shouldn't be able to get most of what you want out of a job. Therefore, you must continually ask the question: 'Do I enjoy what I am doing and does it make me feel good about myself?'

Asking whether what you are doing makes you feel good about yourself is very important. If some of the things you are doing are *not* enjoyable and do *not* make you feel good about yourself, then why are you doing them? It may be understandable if they are actions that will only continue for a short period of time. For example, even though you don't enjoy doing it, you may have to get very involved in a lot of minute detail and have to sort out various complex processes that have gone off the rails. But once you have dealt with the problem you don't have to do those things any longer. We all have to do things that we don't particularly like from time to time. That is just a fact of life. What we are talking about here, however, is a situation where you find yourself consistently having to do things that you don't find rewarding or motivating. Despite what you may believe, you don't have to continue doing those things. There are all kinds of ways in which you can change both the situation and your response to it.

Often the answer to the problem begins to emerge with the second question, 'What should I be doing to be more effective in the job?' The problem, as we know, is that jobs change constantly, but the changes are incremental and we often fail to notice what is happening because we're too close to the situation. And as the demands of the job change, and our behaviour gets more and more out of synch, we feel less and less good about ourselves. The things that worked for us in the past and gave us a feeling of achievement, success and self-worth don't work so well any more, but we're not sure why. You should be reassessing your job, and how you're managing it, two to three times a year at least.

> **"jobs change constantly, but we often fail to notice what is happening"**

The question 'What should I do to manage this job more effectively?' doesn't always result in the answers you want to hear. Sometimes the answers point consistently towards you having to do more and more of what you like less and less. If that's the case, then there's a very important message: this may not be the job for you, and if at all possible you should work towards either changing it or moving to another job. In situations where the behaviour that is required in the job really doesn't suit you, and where it is not motivating you at all, there is a real probability of falling into a downward spiral of negative behaviour. When the behavioural demands of your job are significantly mismatched to the type of behaviour with which you are comfortable – and which you find motivating – blocking behaviour and stress result.

The seven dwarf syndrome

Why do people talk about the Monday blues? Why has Friday become TGIF? Why, in some organizations, do people take so many days off sick? Are they really sick, in the physical sense, or are they just sick of work? In many organizations the instances of people falling ill far exceed the statistical average for the population. However, not all illness is caused by bacteria or viruses. As Molière noted in the seventeenth century, 'The mind has great influence over the body, and maladies often have their origin there'. Sustained high levels of stress can cause physical illness. It is estimated that 75 percent of all illness is stress-related. In the European Union alone 350 million working days a year are lost to stress.

So what is the seven dwarf syndrome? As you recall, the seven dwarfs sang and whistled happily on their way to work. Given that the dwarfs worked underground all day in a mine, what made them so happy that they whistled on the way there? It's easy to understand why they might whistle on the way *back* from work. Snow White was back at the cottage and work was over for the day. But the big question is why did they whistle on the way *to* work?

If you enjoy doing something, you try to do more of it – i.e. you are motivated to do it. The more you do something, generally speaking, the better you become at it. If doing what you like (what motivates you) was a requirement of your job, then presumably you would happily do a lot of it, continue to get better at doing it, and because you were doing it so well you would be rewarded for your efforts. The recognition for doing a good job would make you feel good about yourself and would increase your motivation. You would get a feeling of achievement from your efforts and that would boost your motivation. You would experience a sense of growth as you became more and more expert and effective in your job. And you might be given more responsibility and even get promoted. Having a motivating job leads to a lot of good things.

If you look back at the previous paragraph, you will see that the job we have been talking about offered you all the things that we know to be powerful motivators – achievement, recognition, responsibility, advancement and growth. It allowed you to do what you like doing best; the results you achieved by doing those things were motivating to you; you did more of what you like doing; you got rewarded; and the positive cycle continued onwards and upwards.

Can this sort of thing be achieved? The answer is yes. Behaviour Kinetics shows how. The process begins by looking at a specific job and identifying the key behaviours that are required to manage it most effectively. The next step is to look at what the individual in the job is currently doing. By matching these behaviours with the required behaviours for the job it is possible to identify overlaps and gaps. On the assumption that people tend to do what they like to do and not to do what they dislike doing, the behaviour that an individual exhibits is an indication of what motivates them. If you can then structure a job that requires that behaviour, you have created the seven dwarf syndrome – the individual will whistle on the way to work and Monday will be TGI Monday, while Friday will become ONI (oh no, it's) Friday.

Chapter summary

Motivation is the willingness to exert effort to attain goals. The higher your motivation to achieve a goal, the higher the level of effort you are willing to exert. Motivation is not a personality trait. It's not something you either have or don't have. Nor is it something you may or may not be born with. Everyone is motivated; it just depends by what. When we say someone is not motivated, what we often mean is that they are not motivated to do what we think they should do. Motivation is much more of an inner state rather than something that one person does to another. People are motivated to do things when they want to do them, and when they want to, they'll do them without prompting. Motivation stems from what we are, what we want to be, what we need, and what makes us feel good about what we do. It therefore depends on the individual and the goal.

Pay and good external rewards are adequate to convince employees to spend time with an organization, but they are never enough to convince them to give everything they have to achieve the organization's goals. Motivation comes from things like challenge, recognition for achievement, giving people a feeling of importance, and enabling them to make a meaningful contribution. Compensation and benefits only compensate for the sacrifice of time; they don't engender initiative and going the extra mile.

There is a strong connection between motivation and behaviour. We do things when they are rewarding and pleasurable, and we stop doing, or avoid doing, things when they are unrewarding, disagreeable or unpleasant. We find things that are rewarding and pleasurable motivating and we do them as often as possible. Therefore, if you look at individuals' dominant, repeated behaviour you can make the assumption that this is the sort of thing that they find motivating. The more of these types of things we are able to build into the job, the happier (more motivated) they're likely to become.

There is a great deal of research that supports the fact that what is expected of people – and the way those expectations are expressed – has a major effect on behaviour and performance. The motivational dynamics of expectations involve things like self-esteem, feelings of achievement and other psychic rewards. Because people respond so sensitively to expectations, their ability to read whether those who express the expectations genuinely believe they can be met is highly acute. What we fail to understand is that we tend to be much better at communicating low expectations to people than we are at communicating high expectations. And we also often fail to understand that expectations that are perceived as unreasonable will not be motivating; in fact they will have the opposite effect, rather like the effects of blocking behaviour.

Behaviour Kinetics is helpful in determining what motivates you or others. The first question it asks is 'What are you doing currently to manage your job?' In terms of motivation, the follow-up question is 'Do you enjoy what you are doing and does it make you feel good about yourself?' If it doesn't, you probably don't find it motivating. The third question, 'What should you be doing to be more effective in the job?' raises the issue of whether the job you are in is ever likely to motivate you. If what you should be doing is still not what you enjoy and find rewarding, then find a job that does offer you these things. Life is much more pleasant if you can whistle on the way *to* work.

8

How do you create winning teams?

Build for your team a feeling of oneness, of dependence upon one another, and of strength to be derived from unity. (Vince Lombardi)

We know a lot about what makes teams effective. One interesting bit of research (interesting not only because it is highly off-beat) conducted by Manfred Kets de Vries, is a study of teamwork among pygmies. There are 10 or more pygmy tribal groups living in the Congo-Zaire basin. They are essentially foraging groups whose habitat is hostile and difficult. Effective teamwork is critical for them. Kets de Vries noted that pygmy groups are characterized by seven characteristics. They:

- demonstrate a high level of respect and trust for one another;
- are supportive and protective of one another;
- share common goals;
- hold common values;
- view the individual as less important than the group;
- support completely open communication;
- move leadership between individuals, depending on the situation.

In terms of team effectiveness, the major driver is pressure for performance; the more important the performance of the group, the greater the need for team effectiveness. When both the cost of failure and the reward for success are high, and when both of these are linked to cooperative effort, there is a compelling need to create an effective team. One of the reasons it is often difficult to get professional athletes in individual sports to play together as a team is because they earn stratospheric amounts of money for performing well individually, and the additional reward for making the team succeed has relatively little value. Adequate individual performance maintains monetary compensation within a satisfactory band, and psychic income (sense of self-esteem, feelings of achievement and especially esteem from others) is kept high by media and fan attention and by individual achievements and therefore doesn't act as a major driver for team effort. The added esteem for being a team player is marginal.

What do we mean by a team?

'Team' is one of those words that is used indiscriminately and that has all sorts of meaning and connotations. Almost every group of people in an organization who work loosely together, or sometimes who even work in a common physical area, is referred to as a team. The pre-take-off safety video on a major international airline welcomes passengers as 'part of the team', presumably on the assumption that this invitation will create passenger willingness to watch and listen to the video, and to do what they are told by their 'fellow team members' – the crew.

Size does matter

The short definition of a team is 'a group of individuals committed to a common goal'. The qualifier is that an effective operating team must also be small. The upper size range is generally no more than ten people and there seems to be a consensus among researchers that five to eight works best. The Roman army organized men who lived together, ate together, etc., into groups of eight. In a fighting situation, much as in fluid sports situations, it is important, without having to look around directly for them, to know where your teammates are and what they're likely to be doing. Small teams of people can do that, large groups can't. The issue is interdependency. How can a private soldier feel accountable for the performance of another soldier who, while belonging to the same regiment, may be in a completely different battalion, company and platoon? Harvard professor Richard Hackman says that high-performance teams have 'a collective task that demands a high level of interdependency among [their] members, something that can only be accomplished together'.

In teams in a work environment, research shows that once the size of a group exceeds eight or ten people it tends to fragment into subgroups. Large numbers of people find it difficult to develop the common purpose and commitment required of an effective team. It is also more difficult for them to develop a strong sense of mutual accountability. But if that's the case for working teams, why can sports teams with many more than eight members work closely together and perform superlatively? The answer, of course, is that when you look a little more closely at larger groups like rugby teams, cricket teams, football teams, American football teams, baseball teams and so on, you notice that they are subdivided into specialist groups of players – attackers, defenders, midfield players, bowlers, pitchers, infielders, outfielders, etc. There is an interdependency within the team as a whole, but that is even tighter within the specialist subgroups.

Common goals

The single most important characteristic of effective teams is that every individual in the team feels a deep commitment to a common purpose and common goals. Without this, no team ever attains or sustains a high level of performance.

A number of studies have confirmed that the principal factor characterizing high-performance teams is a commonly held and compelling sense of direction. How do we know this? By observing effective and non-effective teams in action and by taking a Behaviour Kinetics approach and asking them what they think makes the difference. When people in both high-performance teams and poorly performing teams have been asked to describe the current behaviours of the team and what they thought the team should be doing to improve its performance, both groups have consistently highlighted the issue of clear understanding of goals, objectives and direction, and the need for all team members to be strongly committed to them.

Leadership

Leadership plays a significant role in high-performance teams, but leaders would be well advised to heed the principles of Behaviour Kinetics. Individuals who, to paraphrase the Star Trek mission statement, boldly go where the team has not gone before – and perhaps doesn't want to go – destroy team effectiveness rather than creating it. Research shows that directive, authoritative leaders have to be careful of not overplaying their hand. While teams

❝ goals that are imposed rarely attract deep commitment ❞

value having a clear direction and need someone to provide the initiative and stimulus to set the direction, they also want to be made part of the decision-making process. There is a very strong AT ('ask them') element to high-performance teams. Everyone needs to have ownership, and TT ('tell them') doesn't give ownership. The criteria for effective team performance are a deep commitment to a *common* purpose and the sharing of *common* goals. Goals that are imposed rarely attract deep commitment.

Leaders are always role models of one kind or another. That's what people follow. But leaders in high-performance teams have to achieve a delicate balance between modelling a role that the team will engage and follow, and inadvertently projecting a model that is consistently too far out front of the team. Nobody likes to have to play catch-up all the time. Just when you thought you knew the form and you were focusing all your energies on achieving what you thought were the goals, along comes the leader and alters them again. Everyone understands the unique role of the leader and they don't expect them to be able to excel at everything. What they do expect is that the leader will maintain a good grasp of the overall working of the team and enable each member to fulfil their role and contribute their best. Being the star performer who is always out front acting as the lead dog, and who is always 'helping' team members who are not doing what the leader expects, gets in the way of team performance. Taking on all the challenging and rewarding tasks and leaving the less attractive work to the other members of the team isn't leadership, it's self-aggrandisement.

The leadership style that is most effective for creating high-performance teams is a combination of three main things: taking initiative and setting an example, asking for people's input and ideas, and employing full-strength delegation – i.e. being confident in delegating tasks to people and not interfering with them. This is a very difficult behavioural combination to master and we have found it to be relatively rare (slightly less that 20 percent) among the many thousands of managers we have studied and worked with.

Being an AT leader doesn't mean never putting forward any ideas or suggestions. The role of the leader is to lead and that means that the leader has to make some decisions about what others should be doing and what the team should be doing. There is a real, but subtle, difference between initiating goals and objectives and involving people in the process at crucial points. Effective team leadership requires a fine balance between direction and guidance (TT) and consultation (AT), between making critical decisions (TT) and letting others make them (AT), and between control (TT) and delegation (AT). Erring too much on the side of control and direction ('overpowering' TT) undermines innovation, involvement and commitment, but erring too much on the other side ('smothering' AT) and demonstrating no direction, no initiative and no willingness to make hard decisions has the same result.

Role and skill flexibility

At the beginning of its life it is rare to find a team that has all the skills it needs to perform most effectively. However, if the team has a common goal to which all members are committed, people quickly identify the skills that are needed, and develop them. High-performance teams are hothouses of growth, learning and development. Most people have the capacity to focus their attention and learn, but they need the right environment. There are few things quite as motivating as working closely together with a group of people to achieve an important goal. As the team progresses towards its goals, it inevitably comes up against new challenges that require new skills and abilities, and experience with high-performance teams shows they quickly adapt and acquire these skills. An AT environment, combined with a challenge in which everyone is engaged, leads people to stretch their capabilities.

Another characteristic of high-performance teams is the ability to allow and support members to flex their roles and responsibilities to deal with responsibility gaps and overlaps to everyone's satisfaction. One of the problems that haunts ineffective teams is the issue of who is responsible for what. There are often conflicts over whether A or B is responsible for something, or over how a joint responsibility between B and C is to be dealt with, or how to deal with the situation where there is a team responsibility for something but nobody in the team is taking personal responsibility. Low-performance teams are plagued with responsibility overlaps and underlaps. One of the reasons is that low-performance teams tend not to operate in a strong AT mode. Problems remain hidden and often fester and grow, when surfacing them would allow them to be dealt with easily.

Role flexibility is an important ingredient in effective group performance. By role flexibility we mean that the group leadership allows and enables individuals to move into roles where they can add most value. Too often people get pigeon-holed. In one multinational with which we were familiar, once an individual entered a specific function – finance, marketing, sales, production, IT, etc. – they were unable to move to another one. This is not an extreme statement. Over a period of three years of study of this company, we never observed a person successfully managing to move from a role in one business function to a role in another function. Without exception when they made the move they either left the company or were fired within six months. This was silo management at its most extreme, and the company suffered as a result of it.

The absolute opposite of this situation is provided by another multinational company we worked with that adopted a policy of offering all its senior and middle managers the opportunity to decide where they thought they could add most value to the company, and supporting whatever changes they suggested. The rationale for the policy, as the chief executive explained it, was:

Instead of someone in head office, or someone in HR, deciding that Jane Doe should be assigned to head marketing in Djibouti and Fred Bloggs should be sent to run the finance group in Central America, I believe we should ask Jane and Fred where they think they can add most value. Individuals must be given responsibility for their careers and responsibility for delivering the maximum possible value to the company.

A significant number of managers opted to make role shifts that helped them deliver more value, and the company doubled its revenues over a period of a little more than three years. It might be stretching the point to say that the former was completely responsible for the latter, but the policy clearly had a significant impact on the company's growth and profitability.

Role conflict

High-performance teams are clear about each team member's role, even as they flex and change. What made the Roman army units of eight men effective was that each man knew what he was supposed to be doing and what the others were doing, and they were able to move and change their roles as the situation demanded. In teams where roles are rigidly defined, or poorly defined, problems occur. Rigid role definition stifles individuals' ability to acquire new skills and limits the team's capability to deal with changing situations. Poor, unclear role definition often leads to problems of role conflict as two or more people claim responsibility for the same things.

❝ high-performance teams are clear about each team member's role ❞

We witnessed a classic example of role conflict in a company that operated a network of petrol service stations and a network of hotels in Scandinavia. Over the space of several weeks, in various social and business meetings with the top team of the company, we observed that two individuals never spoke directly with one another and never made eye contact. The situation appeared worthy of some investigation and in separate conversations with the two men we learned that one of them was responsible for the petrol stations and the other for the hotels. In many cases petrol stations were located next to the hotels and inns, and the former all had convenience stores, which sold a range of packaged food products, drinks, and even small disposable barbecue sets. They also tended to have picnic areas with umbrellas, tables and barbecues where travellers, particularly families, could rest and eat. The problem was that the next-door hotels operated coffee shops and restaurants and they resented the petrol stations 'stealing' their food business. Because each of the executives was held responsible for his divisional revenue and profitability and not for the revenue and profitability of the team overall, they were constantly in battle with one another and created a negative effect on team behaviour and team performance. The situation was only resolved when areas of both individual and shared responsibility for the two managers were clearly defined and agreed.

Mutual accountability

Where does the buck stop? Unless members hold themselves mutually accountable – that is 'jointly and severally', as lawyers would phrase it, or more colloquially, 'One for all and all for one' – no group ever becomes a team, let alone a high-performance team. Mutual accountability implies a promise from the individual to the team and a reciprocal promise from the team to the individual. 'We're all in this together. If I fail we all fail; if you fail we all fail; if we succeed everyone succeeds.' It's much easier to say than to deliver.

Many organizational teams are comprised of good, earnest, competent, professional people, all of whom are prepared to tackle any task and take individual responsibility for following it through to completion, but few have members who will hold themselves mutually accountable for the team's performance. It's a subtle difference, but an important one. Once again a sporting example comes to mind – the 2004 American Ryder Cup golf team. Each player on the team was/is a consummate professional, an earnest competitor, a highly skilled practitioner dedicated to playing his best, and an individual prepared to take full responsibility for his individual performance. But not, unfortunately, to take responsibility for the performance of the team. There was little sense in the

2004 team that 'If the team play badly I am responsible', or 'If the team play well it's because my colleagues and I have done everything we could to help that happen'.

It might be argued that the failure of the American team and the success of the European team had something to do with the styles of their leaders (or captains). The American style was more TT and the European style more AT. The American captain made his decisions based on what he believed was the best logic. The European captain asked his players for their opinions, listened to what they said, and incorporated their thoughts and ideas into the team game plan.

Mutual accountability cannot be coerced. It is something that develops from a deep commitment to a common goal. But it also requires mutual trust, and trust is something that takes time to develop. When people are introduced to a team they are naturally wary. What are the agendas around the table? Where is everyone coming from? What do they want from me? What do I want from them? What do we all expect from each other? Everyone's been there and everyone knows the feelings. Few people are naïve enough to trust every individual in a group. And if people are essentially rewarded on individual achievement, there is even less incentive or reason to try to build strong bonds of trust.

However, when people really do subscribe to common goals and really do work together to achieve them, trust and commitment develop. An AT style is essential. People need to be consulted; they need to be asked for their views and opinions; they need to feel free to express ideas and suggestions – but they also need to be able to accept it when their suggestions are not adopted, and listen to and buy into the suggestions and ideas of others.

Flying the high cover

Many years ago Harvard Business School did some research into what made front-line staff rank their managers as good or bad. The number one criterion was the degree to which the manager protected the staff from external pressures and sanctions. The researchers didn't go into the rationale, but it probably centres on the fact that pressures that are out of one's control are the most stressful. If your boss says or does something with which you don't agree, you at least have the possibility of engaging them on the issue. If it comes straight to you from your boss's boss it's rapidly spiralling out of your sphere of influence or control. There is a strong correlation between stress and a feeling of powerlessness.

Effective team leaders fly the high cover for their people. They manage a lot of the team's relationships with the outside world, and are expected to do so by both their team members and outsiders. This behaviour insulates the team from having to deal with many of the requests, demands, pressures and irritations to which all working teams are subjected. High-performance team leaders also know when maintaining a safety barrier for the team isn't enough, and when they need to shoot down attackers and blow away the threats and obstacles that are put in the way of achievement. Success has a magnetic effect on people. Everyone wants a piece of it; if they can, they latch on like limpets and attempt to grab some of the credit for themselves. In all types of organizations high-performance teams attract hangers-on who want to take part of the glory but not be part of the hard work. Maintaining the structure and integrity of high-performance teams is never easy; organizations seem to have a destructive urge to bring high performers down to the level of the average.

The high-performance curve

Performance is at the heart of successful teams. In their excellent book *The Wisdom of Teams*, based on research of more than 50 teams in 30 organizations, Katzenbach and Smith conclude, 'The hunger for performance is far more important to team success than team-building exercises, special incentives, or team leaders with high profiles'. A focus on performance creates real teams that deliver top-level results. A focus on *continuous* performance enables them to move through the level of standard results and produce boundary-breaking ideas and solutions.

Katzenbach and Smith talk about a team performance curve that charts the stages that a group of people who begin working together have to go through to become a high-performance team. Their definition supports what we have been talking about: 'A working group relies primarily on the individual contributions of its members for group performance, whereas a team strives for a magnified impact that is incremental to what its members could achieve in their individual roles'.

Most 'teams' in organizations are really working groups and they operate perfectly well. Most 'team building' has nothing to do with creating real teams. It barely scratches the surface of what operating as a high-performance team is about. It is based on the fiction that teams are simply about respect for others and working together. While there is

❝ teams develop by doing, not by playing games ❞

nothing wrong with either of these things, if you want to build a real team then get in the trenches and find out, first, if there is a common goal to which everyone is deeply committed and, second, if they are willing to adopt a common approach to working with clear rules of behaviour. If you can establish those two things, then you can begin the process of working towards the achievement of the common goal and give people the opportunity to assess each other's skills, abilities, reliability, honesty and commitment. Teams develop by doing, not by playing games. Trust in someone doesn't instantly manifest itself by falling backwards with your eyes shut and having them catch you. Artificial games are not the same as real life.

Organizations are structured around roles, and each role has some performance expectation associated with it. Performance management is all about defining expected outputs and activities, applying various techniques to measure the accomplishment of these outputs, and rewarding people on the basis of their level of achievement. In the vast majority of instances, this type of structure reinforces individual behaviour, not team behaviour. Working groups recognize and acknowledge this. Everyone in the group knows that they rise or fall on the basis of their individual achievements. This doesn't mean individuals won't help other people or work with other people. Being a so-called 'team player' simply refers to the idea that everyone in the group is trying to achieve two things: individual success and the achievement of some group target. In many cases the target can't be reached unless everyone cooperates. If marketing doesn't do its job, the sales force can't do theirs. If IT isn't able to make the right information available at the right time, finance finds it difficult to control costs, and production finds it difficult to balance output and maintain quality. If HR doesn't recruit the right people, isn't able to provide appropriate training and development support, or doesn't get the compensation and benefits right, skills shortages occur. This is everyone doing their job and, hopefully, cooperating with everyone else. However, if none of these people take responsibility for results other than their own, they remain a working group, not a team.

A team is created when there is a small group of people who:

- have complementary skills and experience;
- are all deeply committed to a common purpose and goal;
- accept working by a clear set of rules;
- trust one another to do as they say;
- trust one another to do what they can to help every other member of the team;
- accept mutual responsibility for outcomes – 'If you fail, I fail and we all fail'.

A *high-performance* team is created when one further element is added: when every member of the team is committed to the success, growth and development of every other team member. With this added dimension, high-performance teams are able to outperform other teams by a wide margin. The 'all for one and one for all' ethos gets them to punch well above their weight. The key to high-performance teams is actually their ability to get *everyone* to punch above their weight. These teams involve constant encouragement, constant support, complete acceptance, complete honesty, deep trust and an overwhelming desire to achieve success for everyone in whatever way is appropriate. Building a high-performance team is one of the most difficult challenges of leadership.

Chapter summary

Most 'teams' in organizations are really working groups. 'Team-building' exercises and events have very little to do with creating real teams. They barely scratch the surface of what operating as a high-performance team is about. They are based on the fiction that teams are simply about respect for others and working together. Teams develop by doing, not by playing games. The single most important characteristic of effective teams is that every individual in the team feels a deep commitment to a common purpose and common goals. Without this, no team ever attains or sustains a high level of performance.

A team is defined as a group of individuals committed to a common goal. To perform effectively, the team cannot generally be more than ten people, with eight appearing to be an optimal number. Above ten people, teams tend to fragment into subgroups. One of the key elements of a winning team is a feeling of interdependency – one for all and all for one – and the larger the group the more distant this feeling becomes.

Leadership plays a significant role in high-performance teams, but it takes on quite a different aspect in that it tends to be much more distributed among team members. While individuals value having a clear direction for their activities and need someone to provide initiative and stimulus towards setting the team's direction, they also want to be part of the process. There is a very strong AT element to high-performance teams. Everyone needs to have ownership, and TT does not give ownership. Purpose and goals that are imposed rarely attract deep commitment. The leadership style that is most effective for creating high-performance teams is a combination of three main things: taking initiative and setting an example, asking for people's input and ideas, and employing full-strength delegation – i.e. being confident in delegating tasks to people and not interfering with them.

Another characteristic of high- performance teams is the ability to allow and support members to flex their roles and responsibilities. Low-performance teams are plagued with responsibility overlaps and underlaps. High-performance teams are clear about each team member's role, even as they flex and change. Rigid role definition stifles individuals' ability to acquire new skills and limits the team's capability to deal with changing situations. Poor, unclear role definition often leads to problems of role conflict as two or more people claim responsibility for the same things.

Effective team leaders fly the high cover for their people. They manage a lot of the team's relationships with the outside world, and are expected to do so by both their team members and outsiders. This behaviour insulates the team from having to deal with many of the requests, demands, pressures and irritations to which all working groups are subjected.

A team is created when there is a small group of people who:

- have complementary skills and experience;
- are all deeply committed to a common purpose and goal;
- accept working by a clear set of rules;
- trust one another to do as they say;
- trust one another to do what they can to help every other member of the team;
- accept mutual responsibility for outcomes – 'If you fail, I fail and we all fail'.

A *high-performance* team is created when one further element is added: when every member of the team is committed to the success, growth and development of every other team member.

9

How does structure affect performance improvement? Reloading the matrix

Coming together is a beginning; keeping together is progress; working together is success. (Henry Ford)

In the beginning: the hierarchical organization

For a long time after the onset of the Industrial Revolution business needed only to focus on its internal needs. It took raw resources, added labour and some machinery and produced products that it sold. There was no need to worry about pricing strategy or product positioning because competition was limited; there was no need to worry about distribution strategy or retailer clout as there was more than enough shelf space for everyone; and nobody really paid much attention to what consumers wanted – they got what was produced. Henry Ford's famous remark: 'People can have the Model T in any colour – so long as it's black' characterized the situation pretty well.

In these market conditions, work was carried out in a functionally sequential manner and most enterprises organized themselves along functional lines – product development would decide what to make, production would make it, and sales let people know what was available. Sales people did little more than take orders. Organizational structures emphasized command and control, with clear delineation of one-dimensional roles and responsibilities and one-to-one reporting relationships. This is the classic one-boss model. A typical hierarchical organization would have a general manager at the top, with a number of functional direct reports.

As long as the market was not highly changeable and demanding, and as long as the operating environment remained relatively stable, the vertically organized workforce fared reasonably well. The Second World War brought about not only a sea change in political alignment, social values and the balance of global power, it also brought about an unprecedented wave of economic development from a concerted push for new technology to improve productivity and a shift in demography resulting from a generation of war babies. With it came a huge rise in consumption, which in turn spurred more products to enter the market-place, giving consumers more choice, and creating competitive pressures in methods of distribution, in product differentiation and in price. Finally the customer really became king and manufacturers were no longer the dominant force in Western economies. All of a sudden performance, from the top of the organization to the shop floor, became much more important.

Taking care of emerging needs

Paula Martin, CEO of Martin Training Associates, says:

The vertical approach, based on functional goal setting, functional accountability, boss/subordinate performance management and a directive approach to managing, worked well enough until about 20 years ago when we realized that there were some critical components missing from the vertical dimension, the most important of which was the customer. We then realised that in order to satisfy the customer, we had to align with and optimize the horizontal, not the vertical.

Managers came to realize that many business objectives could only be achieved by a number of individuals from different functions working together to complete a process. Matrix organization was born.

The complexity of managing far-flung operations also required organizations to create a structure different from the simple hierarchy. The problem of coordinating resources and objectives across a range of different markets and geographies created a whole new set of problems, such as how to retain overall control at the centre but be able to react to the demands of local cultures and markets. The phrase 'Think global, act local' sounds simple enough, but it's exceedingly difficult to manage in practice.

What is matrix organization?

The matrix organization developed out of the recognition that managing horizontal relations – between groups, functions, departments and business units – was as important as managing vertical relationships. Vertical relationships are relatively straightforward because they are based on power and authority hierarchies. If your boss asks you to do something, you may be more likely to respond because your boss is the person who controls your reward and perhaps your next career move in the organization. Your colleague may have no such power over reward or sanction. But the matrix organization attempts to build authority and responsibility into horizontal

❝ the matrix organization creates the concept of shared responsibility ❞

relationships. It creates the concept of shared responsibility. To get a product or service to market requires the coordinated effort of a number of groups, none of whom have any direct-line authority over one another. However, if they are made to share joint responsibility, then they can all be held accountable, and accountability is a key element in performance.

Everything in a matrix organization is different from the traditional hierarchical model. It is one in which individuals report to more than one individual or group, with different roles and responsibilities in each of the reporting relationships. A simple example is the human resources director of the subsidiary of a global company who operationally reports to the local general manager, but who also reports for technical or functional issues to the human resources director in the region to which the subsidiary belongs. A more complex example is a production manager who is involved in three separate project teams but still retains line-production responsibility.

Few go the whole hog

It is said that the matrix structure originated in the aerospace and defence industries in the 1950s and 1960s. It was adopted to manage complex projects in which many parts of the organization criss-cross each other to get things done on time and within budget. For example, in migrating from a legacy computer system to a new enterprise system, companies often draw on staff from finance, marketing and sales, operations, R&D and information technology departments to form a system implementation team. The team usually works in a matrix structure, with each representative reporting to their respective functional boss, as well as to the project leader.

Many companies also form ad hoc teams to deal with particular issues, such as business process reengineering or a sudden rise in accounts receivables. These task forces come together for a short period of time to solve the problem, with each member going back to their original functional positions once the issue is dealt with. Many consumer product companies have a permanent matrix structure in their marketing and sales departments, with product managers and key account managers forming themselves into relatively stable teams that look after portfolios of products in a range of sales channels.

We have been talking about matrix organizations as if they were pervasive throughout business enterprise, but that's not the case. It is rare that enterprises implement a matrix structure throughout the organization all of the time. Some do so only for certain tasks, some do so only for a period of time, and yet others do it only within certain parts of the enterprise. The reason managers give is that a matrix structure gives rise to complex working relationships and takes a great deal of energy and attention to implement well. The *real* reason is that a matrix structure requires a complete change of behaviour – from a TT culture to an AT culture.

How can a matrix make life easier?

Matrix organizations work well in highly changeable and demanding environments. They do so, first, because they encourage and support innovation. If you think of a project team as a mini-matrix organization, you see how this occurs. The project team is generally given a task that is challenging and unique, in the sense of being something with which the organization has not dealt directly before. Because its members are drawn from different groups and functions, they bring different ideas and viewpoints to the problem at hand. And often the team is freed from restrictive rules and procedures regarding how they are to come up with a solution to the problem with which they are presented. They are given a blue-sky mandate and told to get on with it.

Second, the team is often given freedom to request and acquire resources from anywhere within, and sometimes outside, the company. This creates a free flow of resources that does not exist in a more tightly structure hierarchy. In some sense the team has a licence, if not to steal, at least to borrow what it needs from anywhere. Organization structures work a bit like the human body works. Exercise a muscle the first time and it gets easier to exercise the second time. Open a synapse in the brain and the connection tends to remain. One of the legacies of matrix structures is that they tend to unclog the organization's arteries – the essential flow of communications, ideas and suggestions, innovation and resources. This free flow bridges the critical gap between strategy formulation and execution. The reverse – the stifling effects of rigid bureaucracy – are an organizational form of arteriosclerosis.

ʻʻmatrix structures tend to unclog the organization's arteries ʼʼ

As a corollary to the opening of an organization's resource-flow arteries, a matrix structure also opens up communication across what may have been historically semi-impenetrable boundaries. Networking to get things done within an organization is every bit as important, if not more so, as networking outside. This used to be termed the 'informal organization'. It's the real way things work, as opposed to the way the organization chart says they work. Everyone is familiar with it. In the army it is the sergeants who work it best. In many companies it is the network of secretaries and personal assistants who get things done that otherwise, if they went through the formal channels, would take for ever or end up being blocked. They know the system and they know how to get around it.

How does matrix organization make life more difficult?

The tension inherent in a multi-boss structure easily gives rise to a number of problems, not least because it is complex and unpredictable. It is this last part that really creates the problems. 'Unpredictable' is a manager's euphemism for uncontrollable. Management's darkest and most terrifying nightmares revolve around the fear of losing control. The consultant company A.T. Kearney says that a matrix organization 'violates all of the principles of authority and thereby tends to breed ambiguity and conflict'. To paraphrase Mandy Rice-Davies, one of the principals in a great sex scandal of years ago, 'They would say that, wouldn't they?' A lot of consultancy companies deal in structure and authority and hierarchy. They don't want other types of organizational structures. They support the idea of hierarchy and authority. After all, who makes the decision to hire them and who signs the huge cheques for their advice? You can be pretty sure the decisions aren't a result of an AT consensus and you can also be sure that their advice and recommendations will do nothing to undermine the power and authority of the people who hired them. Virtually all these consulting companies claim to be at the front of the wave in terms of management knowledge, and in a purely technical sense they may be, but if you scratch the surface they haven't really changed their cultures from the principles of management set out by Henri Fayol in 1916 and Lyndall Urwick in 1943, and they have no intention of changing the cultures of their clients either.

Behaviour Kinetics represents a twenty-first century approach to management and organization. It is a major break from the management theories and practices of the first half of the twentieth century. A basic principle of Behaviour Kinetics is that people must be given ownership of change that affects them. Based on AT rather than TT, it is the antithesis of the all-powerful authority hierarchy. It is what makes matrix organization work as it was intended, and it undermines comments such as that of Walter Baber's that 'Matrix organizations seem uniquely plagued with internal conflict because the very concept implies a violation of the principle of unity of command by creating a secondary overlay of authority that contends directly with existing functional authority'. This is the protestation of an anachronistic change reactionary who is clinging to the concept of control and authority at all cost. For an understanding of when unity of command last made sense, go back in time to business as it was described in the first paragraph in this chapter.

What does a matrix structure mean for the manager?

Adopting a matrix structure in an organization has a number of implications for the way managers manage. It requires a different set of management competences, systems and procedures. But most importantly it changes the organization's culture, the most fundamental shift being from TT behaviour to AT behaviour. Without this culture change, matrix organization can only survive in pockets or in highly diluted form. But the senior people in hierarchies reap significant personal gain from their power and position and tend not to be overly keen to give these things up.

Since a matrix structure involves varied and often changing reporting lines and multidimensional working relationships, it is vital that a matrix manager possesses good communication skills and interpersonal skills. In a matrix organization multiple reporting relationships can and do exist. That means that sometimes conflicting objectives have to be balanced by an individual as they try to satisfy different constituencies. However, responsibility does not lie solely with the individual; the structure also requires that the managers to whom they report coordinate their goals and do what they can to make sure they each succeed. Critics condemn matrix organization because they refuse to implement it completely. They continue to try to marry it with traditional hierarchical structures and then wonder why the managers in the system get confused and begin to exhibit mild forms of schizophrenia.

A Behaviour Kinetics approach based on an AT culture means that if there are two or more people to whom an individual reports, they need to discuss with each other what they wish to achieve and then to solicit the input of the individual who reports to them as to how they feel all parties can best be served and all goals best be met. Of course, part of the problem is that the word 'discuss' puts a shiver up many managers' spines. When the word 'discuss' is uttered they hear 'time waste', 'listening to things that don't matter', 'hard work', 'dealing with difficult people and things', and so on. It's so much easier just to tell people what to do.

Getting people to do something involves getting them to change. It means they have to stop doing what they are doing now and start doing something different. Hence every command, order or request implies change. While it may seem 'easier' to a manager to tell people what to do rather than spend time asking them for their ideas and suggestions and discussing with them, it is not necessarily faster. AT and TT are at two ends of a spectrum. They represent two widely different organizational and managerial cultures. AT is probably best characterized as Japanese management and TT as Western management.

For more than a decade, one of our clients was a large US company with worldwide operations. Approximately every two to three years a new management approach or technique, or a new structural arrangement, came issuing down from corporate headquarters. The process was always the same. Teams from head office spread out to the various regional headquarters and presented the new process or structure to the regional senior management. They told the regions what they had to do. Then they repacked their large briefcases and went back home. Shortly thereafter we would be contacted by the various regional groups and would spend the next year or two working with management to get the programmes implemented. Corporate head office spent a couple of weeks doing the telling, so to them it seemed like the fastest and best way to get change implemented. The regions often spent two years to get some degree of acceptance. But even then commitment was rarely

100 percent and quite large pockets of resistance remained. However, the regional people knew very well how the system worked and they made sure that HQ had the impression of full commitment and acceptance from day one.

On the other side of the world the Japanese subsidiary of the company took a different approach. They listened politely to the HQ presentations, thanked the presenters, treated them graciously, and took them to the airport for the flight home. Once again headquarters chalked up a victory for clear presentation, logical thinking and superior intellect. Another win for telling. After the HQ people had been sent packing, the Japanese company began a long series of discussions with the management and staff about the new proposals. Only after a number of months, when everyone had had a say, all opinions had been aired and a general consensus had been reached, was the change rolled out – and, it should be added, successfully implemented, with 100 percent commitment.

This was Behaviour Kinetics at work: ownership of the change distributed to all parties affected; open discussion of current behaviour; open discussion of required new behaviour, inviting the views and opinions of everyone; commitment to change being achieved stage by stage; careful analysis of the effects of changed behaviour; testing and measurement; and – the matrix organization part – involvement of all groups, departments and functions in the consensus.

There is no argument about the fact that the matrix organization requires clear, agreed and well understood guidelines for information flow, resource allocation and conflict resolution. People in a matrix structure need to be prepared to be up-front with issues and be willing to take personal responsibility for resolving them amicably with their peers and bosses. Managers must be confident that, when given responsibility, subordinates will be able to get together and solve problems in the best interest of the company. It is difficult for people to work in a matrix organization without having a reasonable idea of who to talk to, when, and about what. For instance, at some point

" the matrix organization requires clear, agreed and well understood guidelines "

budgets have to be set, agreed and approved. Some system, process and procedure is required to make sure this happens.

Performance evaluation, always a thorny issue for managers, has to be viewed differently in matrix organizations. Measurement is a key element in the process. And agreement to the measures and targets is essential. This is more than management by objectives. MBO has two main weaknesses. First, as Peter Drucker, the man who invented the concept says, 'Management by objectives works if you know the objectives. Ninety percent of the time you don't.' But even assuming clear understanding of objectives, unless the person to whom they apply has at least some degree of input into them (AT) it is unlikely they will be strongly committed. The traditional MBO process is essentially TT, with the boss setting the objectives and the subordinates saying yes, whether they mean it or not.

Making a matrix structure work

Having a matrix structure does not mean appropriate and effective behaviour will follow. All the real work is in getting the people whose names or job titles occupy the spaces on the organization chart to adopt an AT culture.

Stanley Davis and Paul Lawrence (*Matrix*, 1977) suggest that a successful manager of a matrix organization needs to do a number of things, all of which, incidentally, conform to the principles and processes of Behaviour Kinetics. They maintain that an individual needs to:

- learn to work collaboratively;
- develop the ability to use behaviour and expertise as influence instead of formal power and authority;
- be inclusive in decision making – i.e. involve people who are affected by the decision;
- curb impatience with the participative problem-solving process;
- have a balanced orientation towards other functions;
- develop a knowledge of all functional specialties, particularly those that are most complex and uncertain;

■ be able to assess the judgement of the functional specialists and challenge their positions if necessary.

We would add that they should also be sure to:

■ focus purely on behaviour – what people *do*, not who or what they are;

■ focus on asking people rather than telling them;

■ base feedback and evaluation on things that are observable and measurable.

Alan Yu, a friend and colleague whose contributions formed much of the backbone of this chapter, sums up the issue of effective matrix management this way:

It seems that the managers most likely to succeed in a matrix organization need to behave in the same way as good managers in the networked economy of the twenty-first century – supporting in their management style, caring about what others think, winning support for ideas through discussion and persuasion rather than force of authority, and demonstrating the ability to build teams well versed in consensus decision making.

In the multinational corporations I have worked for that have had some success with the matrix structure, we spent an inordinate amount of time on several key activities: aligning the vision of the organization, clarifying roles and responsibilities, laying down the ground rules for decision making and building trust among the players. A matrix is at its best when the participants understand and internalize the behaviour expected of them.

Chapter summary

Aligning objectives and activities vertically is relatively straightforward. Coordinating and integrating people's actions and the results of those actions is a far more difficult task. The problem stems from traditional hierarchical structures. Read almost any but the most recent books on organization and the phrases 'unity of command' , 'line authority' and 'span of control' give you the sense of things. The world of organizations was (and in many cases still is) strongly TT oriented. Probably the factor that has had most influence in driving a change in that model has been the customer. The necessity to integrate the efforts of different departments, divisions and groups in an organization to create a common focus on producing and delivering what customers want, when they want it and at a price they are prepared to pay, has created the need for a different type of structure: the matrix.

Matrix organization does not always work well, and the principal reason is that it requires much more of an AT approach than many organizations are willing to take. The principles of Behaviour Kinetics lie at the heart of successful matrix structures. Liberating people from command and control structures and enabling them to work in the manner of high-performance teams where everybody contributes and everybody cooperates in order to achieve a common goal is what matrix structures should do. Effective matrix structures unclog an organization's essential arteries – communication, ideas and suggestions, resources, innovation – and bridge the gap between strategy and execution.

Adopting a matrix structure in an organization has a number of implications for the way managers manage. It requires a different set of management competences, systems and procedures. But most importantly it changes the organization's culture, the most fundamental shift being from TT behaviour to AT behaviour. Without this culture change, matrix organization can only survive in pockets or in highly diluted form. While it may seem 'easier' to a manager to tell people what to do rather than spend time asking them for their ideas and suggestions and discussing with them, it is not necessarily faster. With an AT approach, time is spent at the front end getting agreement and commitment. With a TT approach the decision is made quickly, but it is often a long time before commitment is achieved and the decision is fully and effectively implemented.

Behaviour Kinetics is the key to effective matrix organization because it demands that a successful manager:

- focuses purely on behaviour – what people *do*, not who or what they are;
- focuses on asking people rather than telling them;
- bases feedback and evaluation on things that are observable and measurable.

10

Making values come alive

Vision without execution is hallucination. (Thomas Edison)

What we value is what we consider excellent, useful or desirable. Values represent the judgement of what individuals or organizations consider is important. They form the basis for how decisions and actions are evaluated. The power of deeply held values is that they determine how individuals act without thinking – how they naturally react to various situations.

The most successful companies don't just have stated values; they link specific behaviours to the values that are observable and measurable. Stated values set out the expectation of specific behaviour. They create both predictability and transparency of behaviour and that provides reassurance to both customers and employees. Trust is the result.

The culture of an organization can be described by its demonstrated core values. For example, Johnson & Johnson's culture is succinctly described by what it calls its Credo. Alan Yu, former managing director of J&J Hong Kong says of the company's values:

The Credo is a document that Johnson & Johnson uses throughout the organization to lay down ground rules for behaviour. Throughout the year, in a variety of locations, executives from different operating companies get together in what is called the 'Credo Challenge'. During these one-to-two-day meetings, the meaning and implications of behaviour consistent with the Credo in cultural and business contexts are debated, and suggestions for amendments to the Credo are recorded. I believe the Credo is one of the reasons why Jim Collins ranks J&J as one of the companies which are 'built to last'.

Research has consistently demonstrated that companies that focus on developing a strong set of corporate values over an extended period of time outperform companies that do not, by a factor of *five to six times*. Companies that are successful over the long term have clear values that are embedded and acted upon by people at all levels. Commonly accepted organizational values create a focused, consistent and unified approach to customers, to markets and to competition. Disciplined and focused energy always triumphs over disorganization and inconsistency.

Continuous performance improvement as a cultural value

For continuous performance improvement (CPI) to work in an organization it must become a core value. It's not a quick fix – something that is done once and then forgotten. It's not a flavour-of-the-month programme that washes through a company, only to be overtaken by the next flavour or fad. It's a long-term process that pays off from the beginning and continues to pay off at an increasing rate as it proceeds.

Toyota Motor Company is the inspiration for CPI. The roots of CPI's development come out of the Toyota Way. Principle 14 of the Toyota Way is, 'Become a learning organization through relentless reflection and continuous improvement'. Jim Collins did not include Toyota in his list of companies that have made the transition from good to great, in spite of the fact that its market capitalization is greater than the combined worth of *Fortune*'s number three and four companies (General Motors and Ford) *plus* Chrysler, simply because it doesn't appear on the Fortune 500 list, and that's where he chose to concentrate his research. But 'relentless reflection and continuous improvement' have enabled Toyota to meet and exceed all Collins' criteria of 'greatness'.

CPI reflects a value of the relentless pursuit of continuous improvement. Recently, Harvard Business School reported the results of research that examined the effects of over 200 well-established management practices on corporate success in 160 companies. In what has to be seen as bad news for instructors in business studies programmes around the world, they found that *none* of these management practices had any direct causal relationship to superior business performance. But what they did find was that there were a small number of basic management practices that, *without exception*, characterized companies that consistently outperformed their industry. Among these were culture and execution. To work, CPI has to become part of an organization's culture – one of its strongly held values – and it has to be consistently applied.

Real values or PR rubbish?

Corporate and individual values are exemplified not by what people say they are, but by what people *do*. You may recall that one of the values that Enron claimed to espouse was 'We treat others as we would like to be treated ourselves'. Perhaps it was operating on the P.T. Barnum code of ethics ('There's a sucker born every minute') rather than an Aristotelian code. But bizarre instances like Enron apart, how often have you heard 'People are our most valuable asset' from any number of companies? And how often have you seen these same companies treat people inconsiderately and shabbily? And it's not just corporations that are guilty; the public service also has a great deal to answer for in this area.

What are your company's values? Are they what the annual report or the PR department says they are? These are not just interesting questions, they are *critical* questions. If you are making the assumption that the people in your organization hold to some stated set of corporate values, then you are assuming that they will behave in a certain manner. If they do not hold a common belief in a set of organizational values, they will behave in widely different ways, some of which will be appropriate and some of which won't. Success cannot result from a whole lot of people pulling in different directions.

❝ success cannot result from people pulling in different directions ❞

The playwright Sir David Hare created a furore with his play *The Permanent Way*, which was highly critical of rail privatization in Britain. When Adrian Lyons, director of the Railway Forum, wrote to him defending privatization, Sir David's reply hit at the heart of the issue of management's stated values and management's behaviour. In his reply to Lyons, Sir David wrote:

As you probably know, the Taiwanese couple who lost their daughter in the Potters Bar crash have – eighteen months later – had no communication at all from Network Rail, no apology, no proper compensation, no inquiry and no explanation. The only contact they have had from anyone at all has been their daughter's ashes, sent to them in an unmarked box with no letter. If you seriously wish to defend a railway system which can treat the bereaved with such stunning and brutal insensitivity, then I suggest you start writing letters to them, not to me.

Values and behaviour

Behaviour reflects values. You can't observe values themselves, you can only observe how they are manifested. It is the *behaviour* of individuals and groups in an organization that shows what its values are. The stated values of Harley Davidson are:

- Tell the truth.
- Be fair.
- Keep your promises.
- Respect the individual.
- Encourage intellectual curiosity.

All these values can be translated into observable, measurable behaviours. It is possible to recognize when individuals are exhibiting truthful behaviour, behaving fairly, keeping promises, showing respect for people, and doing things that encourage intellectual curiosity.

Alcan's corporate values are articulated in greater detail. This is what the company says about them:

Our corporate values guide our growth as a leading, respected and value-driven organization. These values are built on past tradition and form the backbone of our corporate operating philosophy, touching all aspects of our business operations. They guide us as we incorporate economic, environmental and social considerations into our long-term business strategy, daily activities and decisions.

Their corporate values (abbreviated) are:

- ■ *Integrity* – we believe in operating with integrity in all our business dealings.
- ■ *Accountability* – we strive to be openly accountable and willing to align decision-making power with responsibilities at all levels of our organization.
- ■ *Trust and transparency* – we must be transparent in the way we communicate with others, providing timely and accurate information.

Alcan's values can be translated into observable and measurable behaviours. They are real, as opposed to Enron's, which were meaningless doublespeak. Enron's values, as published in their 2000 report were:

- ■ *Respect* – we will work to foster mutual respect with communities and stakeholders who are affected by our operations; we treat others as we would like to be treated ourselves.
- ■ *Integrity* – we will examine the impacts, positive and negative, of our business on the environment and on society, and will integrate human health, social and environmental considerations into our internal management and value system.
- ■ *Communication* – we will strive to foster understanding and support with our stakeholders and communities, as well as measure and communicate our performance.
- ■ *Excellence* – we will continue to improve our performance and will encourage our business partners and suppliers to adhere to the same standards.

We can only hope that Enron's business partners and suppliers did not accept its encouragement and follow its ideas of excellence. Unfortunately 'others' didn't get the chance to treat Enron as it treated them.

Values and excellence

A number of companies do act in accordance with clear values, as Johnson & Johnson and Harley Davidson demonstrate. Hewlett-Packard operated on the basis of very clear values set down by the company's founders. However, the merger with Compaq blurred these values. They didn't describe how the Compaq people thought and behaved. When values are clear, behaviour is predictable; when they become blurred, behaviour becomes erratic.

Proof that the J&J Credo is something by which the company actually lives was provided by the Tylenol crisis in the 1980s. Seven people in Chicago died after taking Tylenol that had been laced with cyanide as part of an extortion plot against the company. Against the advice of lawyers and consultants, who maintained that it would ruin the brand forever, managers at J&J made the decision to remove all Tylenol from the market and to stop all production. The first sentence in the Credo dictated the action: 'We believe our first responsibility is to the doctors, nurses and patients, to mothers and fathers and all others who use our products and services'. The managers took the action while their CEO was on an airplane and could not be reached because they knew it was the right thing to do.

A company's core values define what it stands for. They should spell out what is acceptable and what is unacceptable. They should define the behaviour of individuals and groups. To ignore them is to bring into question the entire corporate culture. People have a perception of an organization that is shaped by what they believe to be its core values – or the lack of them. That perception is confirmed or disconfirmed by their daily dealings with individuals in the organization.

Lou Gerstner says, 'Culture isn't just one aspect of the game, it *is* the game'. Values lie at the heart of a company's culture. What we value is what we reward; what we don't value is what we ignore or punish. Having core values with which everyone in an organization agrees and on which they base their decisions and actions means that managers never have to experience sleepless nights wondering what people 'out there' in the company are doing, or are going to do, about any number of situations. If those individuals 'out there' share the same values as the manager at home base, then they will make similar decisions and take actions similar to those the manager would have taken. Universally strong commitment to core organizational values takes a great deal of stress out of the business of managing. Values determine what you do when you think no one is watching.

❝ values determine what you do when you think no one is watching ❞

A cautionary note: the acid test

So what are your values? Are they congruent with the principles of Behaviour Kinetics? Do you believe that:

1 Behaviour drives performance.

2 The behaviour–performance link is job-specific.

3 The start point for change is acknowledgement of current behaviour.

4 The only true expert is the person who does the job.

5 Ownership of change is essential for success.

6 Change proceeds best from an AT approach, not a TT approach.

7 Successful behaviour change is based on observable, measurable data.

If you don't, then continuous performance improvement is not for you. It's not a gimmick and it's not a catchy fad that will come and go. Those who really want to improve performance continually, to get in front of the wave and stay there, to rise above the crowd, to outperform the competition, and to take the game to a new level will be prepared to internalize the principles of Behaviour Kinetics. They will be prepared to work relentlessly to achieve continuous performance improvement. And they will emerge as the true leaders of our organizations, regardless of their job titles.

There is no practical way of measuring values other than by observing behaviour. Simply asking people to articulate their commitment to values does not produce accurate or satisfactory results. You need to find out precisely what they *do* as they manage their jobs. And, as we have pointed out, if you want to know what people are doing, you have to ask them in a way that enables them to give you a clear and accurate answer, and this implies using some type of carefully designed diagnostic questionnaire.

The technology of 360° feedback and assessment is one way of going about it. Because it is often difficult for people to be objective about what they do, the 360° process is helpful in that it allows for objective feedback from individuals who observe the subject as that individual goes about the job. If done well, 360° feedback can show the degree to which an individual exhibits a number of behaviours.

The downsides of 360° processes are that it tends to require a lot of time from a lot of individuals. Also, if it is to focus on specific behaviours, it must, by definition, limit the behaviours to a smallish number, otherwise the questionnaires become tremendously cumbersome and their cost/benefit ratio becomes negative. Using a validated individual diagnostic that measures a wide range of *specific* behaviours is clearly an easier way to achieve the objective.

Assessing commitment to corporate values

Using a Behaviour Kinetics approach, it is possible to assess the degree to which individual members and groups within an organization actually believe in and demonstrate its core values. It's an AT process. First, it defines the behaviours that reflect core values and then it asks people to identify what they are currently doing and compares their behaviours with these stated values. The example that follows is taken from a communications company that, having grown rapidly through mergers and acquisitions, agreed that it needed to establish a set of core values to which all employees could subscribe.

Recognizing that its different business units were being driven by diverse sets of values, and that this situation was leading to unnecessary conflict and disagreement, senior management invited input from a wide range of managers and staff. The result of this process was a defined set of core values. These were articulated as:

- Being a straight arrow.
- Being passionate about the job.
- Thinking outside the box.
- Delivering quality and commitment.

The values were explained and elaborated to some degree in a booklet that was distributed to all staff. This was followed by a series of presentations, speeches, meetings and workshops setting out and discussing the values. However, quoting Lou Gerstner again, 'You can't simply give a couple of speeches or write a new credo for the company and declare that a new culture has taken hold'. Senior management recognized that presentations and meetings would have some effect – that they would at least resonate with a number of individuals and groups who were ready to buy into the values – but they also recognized that a large number of people would not agree at all or only partially buy in.

The company recognized that if it asked people directly about their commitment to the set of core values it would be highly unlikely to find any who would say that they should *not* be straight arrows (being open and honest with colleagues and customers), should *not* be passionate about the job (being deeply committed to the goals of the company and creating a climate of enthusiasm, inspiration and a desire to succeed), should *not* try to think outside the box (challenging established ways of doing things, testing processes and systems for their ability to add value) and should *not* deliver quality and commitment (taking responsibility to deliver a quality output first time, every time). What they did instead was ask people about their *behaviour* – what they were currently doing to manage their jobs.

Peter Drucker maintains that in any change initiative 10–15 percent of people in an organization will be supportive from the outset, 10–15 percent will be adamantly opposed and the rest will be uncommitted. It is the uncommitted for whose hearts and minds it is necessary to compete. Once a significant momentum for change has been established, the uncommitted increasingly come off the fence and become supporters of the change. As the tide of support grows larger and larger, some of the strong resistors become converts. However, there are always die-hards who will resist to the very end. The ultimatum they eventually face is probably best described by the great American football coach Vince Lombardi, after whom the Super Bowl Trophy is named: 'If you aren't fired with enthusiasm, you will be fired with enthusiasm'.

The measurement process

Step 1

The first step was to articulate clearly what each of the four core values actually meant.

- 'Being a straight arrow' means:
    - being open and honest with colleagues and customers;
    - creating relationships based on trust and respect;
    - recognizing people for who they are and what they achieve;
    - helping people to be the best they can be;
    - supporting people's ideas and efforts.
- 'Being passionate about the job' means:
    - being deeply committed to the goals of the company;
    - creating a climate of enthusiasm, inspiration and a desire to succeed;
    - having pride in the job and in the company;
    - taking ownership of problems and accepting responsibility for both success and failure.
- 'Thinking outside the box' means:
    - challenging established ways of doing things;
    - testing processes and systems for their ability to add value;
    - encouraging and listening to all suggestions and ideas;
    - never dismissing an idea without giving it real consideration.
- 'Delivering quality and commitment' means:
    - taking responsibility to deliver a quality output first time, every time;
    - paying attention to detail and being absolutely reliable;

- always delivering on promises;

- always meeting deadlines;

- always making sure the customer is satisfied.

Step 2

The second step was to take each of these component parts of the value definitions and identify a set of specific behaviours that described them. For example, for the component parts of the definition of 'Being a straight arrow', a total of 37 specific, observable, measurable behaviours were identified. They were as follows:

■ Being open and honest with colleagues and customers (measured by 6 behaviours):

- letting people know where you stand on things;

- giving and seeking clear and honest feedback;

- giving people frequent feedback on performance;

- never failing to keep a commitment;

- always treating people with respect;

- being open and available to people.

■ Creating relationships based on trust and respect (measured by 12 behaviours):

- actively soliciting suggestions and opinions;

- encouraging and supporting people's ideas;

- accepting failure if effort and intent were genuine;

- not interfering once you have delegated something;

- helping people overcome pressure in their jobs;

- giving people authority to change the way they do things;

- working for a win-win resolution to conflicts;

- dealing directly and openly with performance problems;

- treating people fairly;

- giving people visible recognition for their achievements;

- trying to support people through their difficulties;

- being loyal and supportive to colleagues.

■ Recognizing people for who they are and what they achieve (measured by 11 behaviours):

  - giving people recognition for ideas and suggestions;
  - encouraging people to accept challenges;
  - allowing people to demonstrate their skills and abilities;
  - giving people visible recognition for their achievements;
  - focusing on achievement and results, not effort;
  - giving people tasks that suit their skills and abilities;
  - making sure people get the resources they need to do their jobs;
  - helping people learn and progress in their jobs;
  - encouraging and supporting people's ideas;
  - trying to drive decision levels downwards as much as possible;
  - getting people to determine how they can best add value.

■ Helping people to be the best they can be and supporting their ideas and efforts (measured by 8 behaviours):

  - encouraging people to accept challenges;
  - getting people involved and enthusiastic about things;
  - encouraging people to be proactive rather than reactive;
  - encouraging people to take considered risks;
  - giving people authority to change the way they do things;
  - encouraging and supporting people's ideas;
  - allowing people to excel;
  - getting people to think about what they can do best.

Step 3

At this stage, enter Behaviour Kinetics. It's AT time: time to ask people to identify their current behaviour. Staff across the company were asked to complete a diagnostic questionnaire that enabled them to identify the whole array of their specific job behaviours.

Step 4

The fourth step was the analysis of the data. Analysis focused on the specific behaviours deemed to reflect the company's core values. This analysis enabled an assessment of the degree to which individuals, teams, groups, divisions and the company as a whole exhibited these specific behaviours in their daily work. Each of the behaviours was quantified on a scale of 0–10. They were then grouped by core value and the degree to which managers were seen to be demonstrating each of the four core values was also calibrated on a scale of 0–10. The acceptable level of behaviour was set at 7.5.

Analyzing the data

Values-related behaviour at the company level

Figure 10.1 shows the scores for each core value across the organization.

The overall results indicate that the largest gaps between the company's hoped-for level of value acceptance and its actual level are in the values

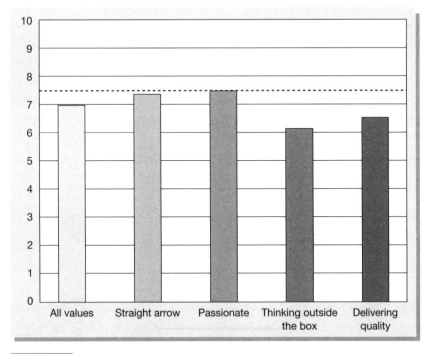

Figure 10.1   Core values chart: whole company

'Thinking outside the box' (with a score of 6.2) and 'Delivering quality and commitment' (with a score of 6.5). The other two core values, 'Being a straight arrow' and 'Being passionate about the job' are being exhibited across the company as a whole at or very near to the targeted level of 7.5.

This is the overall picture, but as we all know, averaging large amounts of data hides possibly wide variances. The point of the exercise was to find out where the core values were being demonstrated and to identify the pockets within the company where they were not. The analysis proceeded down through the organization, from company to divisions, to departments, to work groups and teams, and finally to individuals.

Values-related behaviour at the divisional level

At the divisional level the data began to show some degrees of variance. Figures 10.2, 10.3, 10.4 and 10.5 show the differences in the degree to which the core values were demonstrated by managers in four of the company's six divisions.

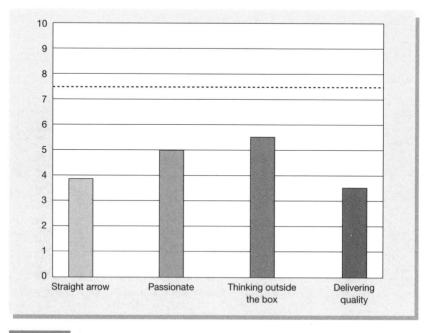

Figure 10.2 Core values chart: Division 1

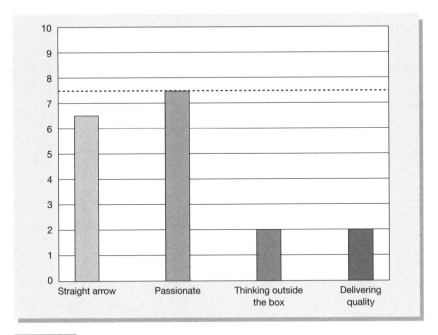

Figure 10.3 Core values chart: Division 2

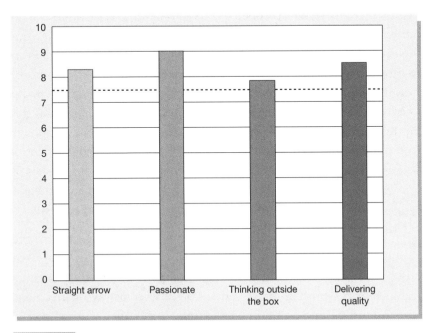

Figure 10.4 Core values chart: Division 3

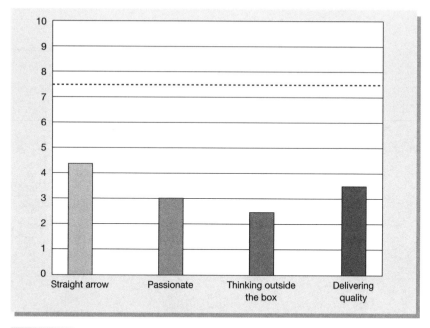

Figure 10.5 Core values chart: Division 4

As these charts show, acceptance of the company's core values varied rather dramatically between divisions. Generally speaking, the four divisions represented companies, or parts of companies that had been acquired. But regardless of the historical background, the clear message was that a large number of individuals and groups were only paying lip service to the company's core values, or, as the popular expression has it, 'Talking the talk but not walking it'. All the presentations, pamphlets and inspiring speeches had been unable to change that. Lou Gerstner's words warrant repeating: 'You can't simply give a couple of speeches or write a new credo for the company and declare that a new culture has taken hold'.

❝ people may sometimes be difficult but they aren't stupid ❞

Without a reliable means of measuring the degree to which values have been integrated into the way a company is run, talk about core values remains just that – talk. In the 1990s British Airways spent a huge amount of time and effort on a programme they called 'Putting people first'. It was essentially an attempt to instil a set of values around treating people as a highly valued asset. However, the behaviour of management ran in direct contradiction to the stated value, and the slogan became a source of derision within the company. 'Putting people first' was all talk and no action. People may sometimes be difficult but they aren't stupid.

Values-related behaviour at the department level

Moving the analysis down a level within Division 2, once again there are wide variances of values-related behaviour (see Figures 10.6 and 10.7). Department B is quite clearly not on the same values wavelength as their colleagues in Department A. The objective of the analysis is to help pinpoint where to focus time and energy on trying to get buy-in to the core values – and Department B surfaces as one of the hot-spots that requires attention.

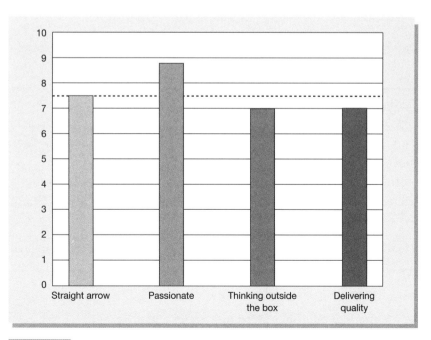

Figure 10.6 Core values chart: Division 2, Department A

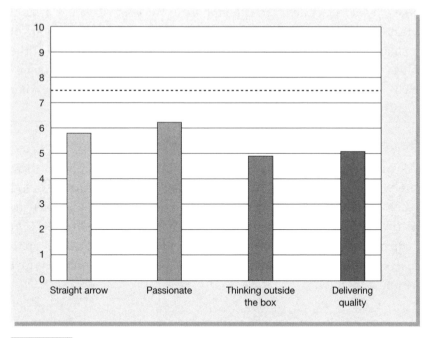

Figure 10.7   Core values chart: Division 2, Department B

Values-related behaviour at the team level

Taking the analysis a step further, it is possible to examine the behaviour within teams and determine the degree to which they support the company's core values. As an example, we can look at one of the four subcomponents of the core value 'Thinking outside the box' –'Challenging and testing processes' – and examine how the various teams in Department A demonstrate the six specific behaviours that are deemed to reflect it.

'Challenging and testing processes' is demonstrated by the following six specific behaviours:

- cutting red tape wherever possible;
- questioning the value added by systems and processes;
- encouraging people to take considered risks;
- always looking for the better way to do things;

■ never being satisfied with current achievement;

■ changing the way work is organized.

Figure 10.8 shows how these behaviours were demonstrated by four teams within a division. Once the company has this data, each team can be approached in a different way, focusing on different priorities. If a behaviour is being exhibited to a satisfactory degree, it can be reinforced, but it does not require large amounts of management time or energy. However, if a behaviour supporting an important component of a core value is not present to a significant degree, then it merits resources and attention.

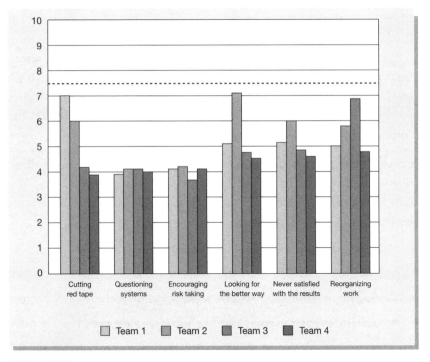

Figure 10.8 Core values subcomponents chart: Department A, Teams 1, 2, 3, 4

Value-related behaviour at the individual level

Mining the data down to the smallest organizational unit brings us to the behaviour of specific individuals. Once again, if workshops, meetings, discussions or one-to-one coaching are going to be used to move behaviour toward the core values, from the company's point of view it is important to know where to focus resources. Large-scale change programmes tend to have rather patchy results. You have probably had experience with one or more of them. There are a number of reasons for their general failure, but one of them is that the change is often introduced through a series of meetings or workshops that blanket everyone in the organization. It is what might be termed a 'sheep dip' approach. Everyone gets dipped, whether they need it or not. Some people need no dipping and some need to spend more time in the pool, but it's one-size-fits-all and everyone gets the same treatment. It's patronizing and annoying to those who don't need it and a waste of effort for those who need greater attention.

Individuals all have different patterns of behaviour. They do different things as they try to manage their jobs effectively. Most people want to do as good a job as they can. They want to do the right things rather than the wrong things. It's not altruism towards the company, it's a matter of both self-esteem and self-preservation: do the wrong things for long enough, however they're defined, and your career in the company comes to a sudden halt.

Core values data on individuals allows a company to tailor values-related training and development to the needs of individuals. The following personal scores are a sample of the output for an individual we shall call Simon Winsor.

- Being a straight arrow (overall score 6.7):
  - being open and honest with colleagues and customers 6.0
  - creating relationships based on trust and respect 6.5
  - recognizing achievement and helping people excel 7.2
  - supporting ideas and effort 6.9
- Being passionate about the job (overall score 6.8):
  - being committed to the company's goals and creating a desire to succeed 7.9
  - having pride in the job and in the company 6.0
  - taking responsibility and owning problems 6.4

■ Thinking outside the box (overall score 7):

    – challenging and testing established processes   6.7

    – encouraging and listening to suggestions   7.3

■ Delivering quality and commitment (overall score 5.3):

    – paying attention to detail   5.3

    – meeting deadlines   5.3

Figure 10.9 shows how his scores compared with those of his team.

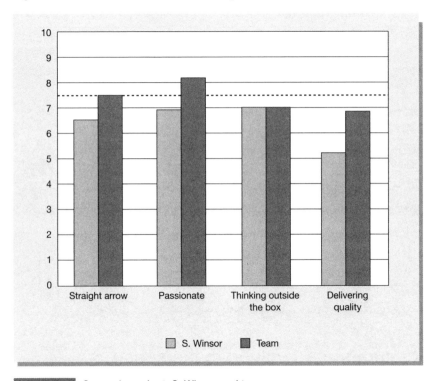

Figure 10.9 Core values chart: S. Winsor and team

As well as these overall scores, Simon was given detailed feedback on specific behaviours that are deemed to demonstrate each of the core values. For example, his results for the core value 'Being a straight arrow' included the following:

■ Creating relationships based on trust and respect:

    – actively soliciting suggestions and opinions   8

- encouraging and supporting people's ideas   6
- accepting failure if effort and intent were genuine   8
- not interfering once you have delegated something   6
- helping people overcome pressure in their jobs   9
- giving people authority to change the way they do things   7
- working for a win-win resolution to conflicts   2
- dealing directly and openly with performance problems   4
- treating people fairly   5
- giving people visible recognition for their achievements   6
- trying to support people through their difficulties   9
- being loyal and supportive to colleagues   8

■ Supporting ideas and efforts:

- encouraging people to accept challenges   9
- getting people involved and enthusiastic about things   9
- encouraging people to be proactive rather than reactive   1
- encouraging people to take considered risks   7
- giving people authority to change the way they do things   8
- encouraging and supporting people's ideas   6
- allowing people to excel   8
- getting people to think about what they can do best   6

Make sure stated values make sense

Lots of stated values are just that – stated but not really intended to be acted upon. They are often there for the decoration. It's like Mom, Apple Pie and Father Christmas; it's difficult not to support them even if you never liked your mother, you're highly allergic to apples and you have never got over the terror of being held on the lap of an old man in a false white beard who breathed whisky fumes over you and surreptitiously stroked your leg. Sometimes a statement of values appears in organizational documents simply because it has to. Creating statements of values is an industry. We started out with the fashion must-have of mission statements and once the genie had been let out of the bottle it had to be fed with other kinds of 'statements'. Corporate fashion is every bit as real as dress fashion.

Corporate value statements are more often TT than AT. Someone or some group somewhere comes up with a set of values that are deemed to be what the organization stands for. It's not very difficult to make them up. What do you think the values of the prison service, the refuse collection service, the healthcare system, a top-level sports team, a nuclear power plant, the army, a children's charity, the mafia, a political party, a church, a bar, or a car dealership should be? You can make it into a rather amusing game; everyone writes down what they think the values of any individual or group should/could be and then they share their answers. If you don't believe people are creative, wait until you try this game.

Rather than just telling people what their organization's values are, and then telling them again and again in the hope that repetition will bring acceptance, there is a better approach. It applies the principles of Behaviour Kinetics, and a great example is how, upon becoming CEO of IBM, Sam Palmisano approached the issue. Using the company's communications technology, he asked all of IBM's 320,000 employees, spread across 170 countries, to contribute their thoughts on what they thought the company's core values should be. The process generated a million words, and these were boiled down into a set

❝ it's not what people *say* they believe that matters, it's what they *do* ❞

of values that, like the Johnson & Johnson Credo, now form the basis for how operational decisions are made by IBM employees worldwide. There is complete commitment to these values because everyone was involved and every one of the 320,000 IBMers had a say.

The message is that if you're going to create a statement of values for other people you'd better make sure it makes sense to them and that they can, with the application of some AT process, commit to it. And the only way to measure values is to observe and measure behaviour. It's not what people *say* they believe that matters, it's what they *do*.

Chapter summary

Research shows that companies that focus on developing a strong set of corporate values over an extended period of time outperform companies that do not by a factor of five to six times. Commonly accepted organizational values create a focused, consistent and unified approach to customers, to markets and to competition. However, many stated corporate values are simply a PR exercise and don't reflect reality. One of the reasons is that values statements are an organizational 'must have'. They're fashionable. But because creating commitment to common values takes hard work, companies often just invent a set of statements and either leave it at that or hope that by repeating them over and over again they will come to be accepted.

There is, of course, another way to create common core values. It involves applying the principles of Behaviour Kinetics. Outstanding examples of how this approach leads to creating powerful values that have real meaning to everyone involved are Toyota, Johnson & Johnson and IBM.

Two of the fundamental principles of Behaviour Kinetics are adopting an AT approach and focusing on observable, measurable behaviour. Assessing whether values are real – i.e. form the basis for people's actions – or are little more than talk, requires measurement and there is no practical way of measuring values other than by measuring observable behaviour. Asking people whether they are committed to values is not good enough; it's not what they say that matters, it's what they do.

Measuring the degree to which values are internalized is a relatively straightforward process. It involves the use of behavioural technology in the form of questionnaires that determine specifically what people are doing as they manage their jobs. Values need to be translated into behavioural terms. Commitment to a value (e.g. 'Creating relationships based on trust and respect') manifests itself in a number of behaviours. If you do these things then it is a clear demonstration that you subscribe to the value. If you don't do these things then it almost certainly means you don't. Any organization that is serious about its values needs to look at how its people are behaving. Actions, not words, tell the story.

11

The process of continuous performance improvement for an individual

Most of us have jobs that are too small for our spirits. (Studs Terkel)

All performance improvement and all organizational change begin with individuals. In their book *Leading Strategic Change: Breaking Through the Brain Barrier*, Black and Gregersen argue that the commonly accepted approach to change is wrong. It takes what they call an 'organization in' approach, meaning that it begins by identifying the organizational levers that will make individuals follow a change plan and then it drives that plan down through the company. This sounds very much like TT. Black and Gregersen point out that 'Lasting success lies in changing individuals first; then the organization follows. An organization changes only as far or as fast as its collective individuals change.' When individuals in a team change their behaviour, the team changes; when teams change the way they operate, they impact on the way others operate. A culture of continuous performance improvement is built one piece at a time. This doesn't mean the pieces can't be put together very rapidly or that the change can't be spread quickly, but the basic building block is the individual, and each individual must be approached on an AT basis and given ownership of the process. People change when and how they want to, not when and how others want them to.

As we pointed out in Chapter 1, big-bang change has a very mixed success record. It is almost always 'organization in' and is driven down through the organization, which means that the change is externally determined and there is very little room for individuals to have any input. The majority of books and articles about overcoming resistance to change are focused on big-bang change programmes. Newton's third law of motion states that for every force there is an equal and opposite force. For instance, if you push on a wall it will push back on you as hard as you are pushing on it. This law also tends to apply to big-bang change; the harder you push for change, the harder the resistance to change pushes back. One of the reasons, of course, is that big-bang change tends to be heavily TT-oriented. It is generally imposed change and human beings have a natural tendency to resist imposed change. They bridle at being forced to do things with which they don't agree, or over which they have no influence. To manage change successfully, you have to take a very different approach.

Continuous performance improvement on a personal level

Change is generally incremental, so effective adaptation to change should be correspondingly incremental. Ideally, you should change your behaviour in synch with the changes in your job or role. This implies that you are able to be consistently aware of how your role is changing, and that's not always easy. It requires constant attention, and it takes time and effort. Unless we see clear returns, we are all reluctant to expend time and effort on something. Keeping close track of small changes in your job is the sort of activity that encourages procrastination. 'Things don't appear to have changed that much and so it really won't make any difference if I take time to step back now or next month to analyze what, if anything, has happened. Besides, I think I'm pretty well on top of things. I'll get back to this when things really have changed.'

> **❝ change is generally incremental, so effective adaptation to change should be correspondingly incremental ❞**

But if that's what you think, there is a large group of people who will tell you that you're absolutely wrong. They are individuals who go through a process two or three times a year that allows them to analyze the myriad and often imperceptible changes that have occurred in their jobs and enables them to adjust their behaviour accordingly. They are constantly, like expert surfers, on top of the performance wave. They continue to deliver optimal results month in, month out. We call the process CPI (continuous performance improvement) and we describe how it works in this chapter.

The CPI process

The CPI process works because it is based on Behaviour Kinetics. The necessity for hard behavioural data is at the heart of Behaviour Kinetics. Unless you are able to determine precisely, in observable, measurable, behavioural terms, what people are doing and what they think they should be doing differently, performance improvement – let alone *continuous* performance improvement – becomes a random process. This information cannot be obtained any other way than through the use of scientifically and rigorously constructed behavioural diagnostic questionnaires. As we know, simply asking the question 'What are you doing now and what should you do differently to improve your performance?' does not produce clear and detailed answers. The questions have to be asked in a way that enables people to provide clear and articulate responses.

Being based on the principles of Behaviour Kinetics, CPI does the following things;

1 It focuses purely on behaviour because performance is driven by behaviour. Personality predicts less than 10 percent of performance.

2 It is job-specific because effective job performance depends on the behavioural demands of the particular job. There is no list of generic behaviours that consistently lead to top-level performance.

3 It begins by establishing, through an AT process, the specific behaviours that individuals and groups are currently exhibiting. It enlists the aid of behavioural technology to do this.

4   It enables individuals and groups, once again through an AT process and with the aid of behavioural technology, to recognize what they need to do to improve their performance.

5   It creates a non-emotional, non-evaluative agenda for discussion of performance improvement, based purely on observable behaviour.

6   It takes the threat out of behaviour feedback. The data reflect what individuals observe about themselves. They own it. It is not the opinion of third parties.

7   It is based on information that is observable and measurable. This enables the progress of change to be constantly monitored.

The CPI process involves a series of steps, as shown in Figure 11.1.

1   **Benchmarking current behaviour and performance**. The CPI process begins with individuals completing a diagnostic questionnaire that enables them to see precisely what they're doing – the *specific behaviours* to which they are currently giving greatest priority and emphasis in the management of their jobs.

2   **Acknowledgement of current behaviour and reinforcement of ownership**. Having been presented with a list of the specific things they're currently doing to drive performance in their jobs, it's necessary to get people to internalize this data, accept it and take full ownership of it. To do this, they are asked to identify how they actually demonstrate each of their top-priority behaviours. For example, in explaining how she demonstrates the behaviour 'Create integrative processes and systems', one manager describes her actions this way:

   ▪ In designing solutions for the customer, I seek to involve input from the organization's finance and operations departments and spend much time listening to their input.

   ▪ I make a point of discussing my experience of industry developments with others in the organization who will find the information relevant.

The point of this exercise is twofold. First, it reinforces the fact that these are indeed the behaviours to which the individual is currently giving greatest priority and emphasis – i.e. it reinforces acceptance

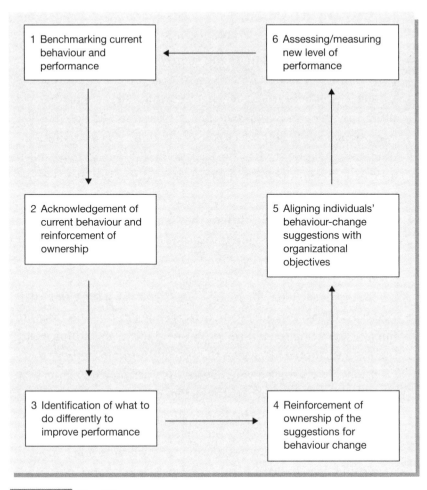

Figure 11.1   The CPI process

and ownership. About 20 specific behaviours account for about 80 percent of one's results. Second, it forces the individual to think about how to make these behaviours visible to others. Unless people see clearly what you're doing, how can you expect your actions to have any effect? In many cases managers believe that people will somehow just 'know' what they intend, will know what their objectives are, will understand the strategy, and will know what behaviour and results are required of them. This can only be described as a belief in management by transmogrification – which is a fancy way of saying magic. For behaviour to have an effect on performance, it has to be visible and recognizable.

3 **Identification of what to do differently to improve performance.** A second function of the diagnostic questionnaire is to enable people to articulate what they think they should be doing differently in order to improve their performance. Because it is exceptionally difficult for us to be able to bring up to the front of our brains what we have in the back of our minds and to be able to articulate these thoughts and ideas clearly, once again behavioural technology is required.

4 **Reinforcement of ownership of the suggestions for behaviour change.** The CPI process reinforces the fact that the list of proposed performance-improving behaviours is what the individual is suggesting, not what anyone else suggests. It establishes clear ownership of the ideas for change. There is no guarantee that the suggested behaviours are precisely the actions that are necessary to improve performance, but we know one thing: people think more highly of their own ideas than they do of the ideas of others, and we believe Peter Drucker when he says the person who knows best how to do a job is the person in the job. If it's your job and these are your suggestions then (a) they're probably pretty accurate, and (b) you're more likely to consider them seriously. What you do about them becomes your responsibility. Ownership and responsibility go hand in hand.

5 **Aligning individuals' behaviour-change suggestions with organizational objectives.** Earlier on we skipped over this problem by saying that the answer was to blend the input of individuals with the objectives and requirements of the organization in as flexible and open a manner as possible. True, but perhaps not overly helpful. The CPI process is much more specific. By getting individuals' managers to complete a behavioural diagnostic that enables them to articulate the specific behaviours they think are critical for managing the subordinate's job effectively, the CPI process structures a discussion between boss and subordinate that does two things:

■ It focuses the discussion purely on behaviour. It therefore avoids all the pitfalls of discussion of things like attitude, motivation, personality, etc.

■ It builds on agreement between the boss and the subordinate rather than on differences. This is because the lists of what the manager thinks are important always contain a degree of match with the behaviours that the subordinate is either demonstrating currently or believes they should be demonstrating to improve performance. We have never come across an instance where this has not been the case.

An example of CPI

1 Identifying current behaviour

We shall illustrate the CPI process with the case of a specific individual. Her name is Roberta Webb. She works for a multinational electronics firm. Her job title is Finance Manager, Eastern Europe. The countries that come under her remit are the Czech Republic, Hungary and Romania. She has been in her job for 10 months. Prior to that she worked for a large aerospace company. Her performance is rated good but there are some concerns about her difficulty in getting changes implemented across the region. She is aware of these concerns and shares them. Her company has bought into the concept of CPI and is involving their entire European management team in the process. As a result we shall be able to demonstrate the implementation of the CPI process as it moves from the individual (Roberta) to the team (Eastern European Finance Team), to the company, and how the company maintains and reinforces its core values throughout.

CPI focuses purely on behaviour, and the first stage in the process is to get people to identify the specific things they do as they manage their jobs. So what is Roberta doing to manage her job at the moment?

Being an AT process, we begin by asking Roberta to complete a diagnostic questionnaire called 'Momentum CPI'. It identifies and quantifies approximately 400 specific work behaviours. Her results are then fed back to her in a one-to-one meeting. First, here are the 20 specific behaviours she is currently using most as she manages her job. (They are set out in groups of five simply because lists of five things are easier for the brain to cope with than lists of 20 things). Her performance-accelerating behaviours are in plain text and her *performance-sustaining behaviours* are shown in italics. She:

- Leads change by setting the example.
- States arguments persuasively.
- *Breaks broad targets down into areas where action can be taken.*
- *Simplifies complex problems for people.*
- *Takes things through to completion.*

- Confronts difficult decisions.
- Helps people to learn from their mistakes.
- Accepts responsibility for all outcomes, good or poor.
- Gets people committed to common objectives.
- Constantly suggests ideas for how to improve performance.

- *Makes sure people don't fail because of lack of appropriate resources.*
- *Helps people overcome pressures in their jobs.*
- *Lets people know how they are being evaluated.*
- *Always treats people with respect.*
- *Sets and focuses on the priorities.*

- *Thinks changes through carefully.*
- *Helps people develop the necessary skills for their jobs.*
- *Stresses the need for careful planning.*
- Gets people to flag how they can best contribute to team performance.
- Clears away obstructive processes and procedures.

(As mentioned in Chapter 4, the decision as to whether a specific behaviour either accelerates or sustains performance is not subjective. It is based on the views of 5,000 or so working managers.)

2 Acknowledging the behaviour and reinforcing ownership

Remember that the 20 behaviours on the list above are what *Roberta* has said she does most. She *owns* this output. It isn't someone else's view of her behaviour; it's hers. This is hard data, and it's not evaluative in terms of being good, bad or indifferent. It's simply the fact. To reinforce that, once the list has been given to Roberta, the next step in the CPI process is to ask her to think about each of the behaviours and (a) make a note of two or three recent instances when, and in what context, she did these things, and (b) to write down specifically what she did that allowed other people to recognize what she was doing – i.e. how she actually demonstrated each behaviour. For example, Roberta attempts to make the behaviour 'Simplifies complex problems' visible to people by, as she phrases it, 'discussing comparable situations where a similar problem was addressed previously, and flow-charting logical steps in analyzing the problem'.

This process does two things. It allows Roberta to acknowledge her behaviours, and it raises the issue of the 'why' of the behaviours – why she did what she did when she did it, and what the perceived consequences were.

3 Identifying any blocking behaviours

Once Roberta has thought through and accepted what she is currently doing to both accelerate and sustain performance, the next step is to feed back to her what she says she is doing that may be blocking performance. Blocking behaviour is neither exceptional nor unusual. Most of us exhibit performance-blocking behaviours from time to time because life in any organization is fraught with various frustrations, anxieties and uncertainties. There are very few people who don't react to these things.

Here are the blocking behaviours that Roberta says she exhibits to a noticeable degree (i.e. to a degree where others working for her would acknowledge that she does these things). She:

- Tends to look the other way rather than deal with performance issues.

- Shows her anger with people when they fail to do what is expected of them.

- Backs away from taking on additional responsibility.

- Tends to be openly critical of others.

- Avoids stating her position in arguments.

- Tries to avoid making decisions on potentially controversial issues.

- Is reluctant to give negative feedback.

- Tends to bend the rules to keep the peace.

4 Acknowledging blocking behaviour and reinforcing ownership

Once this list has been given to Roberta, the next step in the CPI process is to ask her to think about each of these behaviours and try to recall, and then write down, (a) when she recently did each of these things, and (b) what *caused* her to do them. The key issue with blocking behaviour is its cause. Blocking behaviour is not personality driven, it's situation driven. It is a reaction to an occurrence that is in some way threatening, frustrating, confusing, demeaning, aggressively challenging, etc. Because it's a reaction to an external stimulus, if you can identify the stimulus and eliminate it, the reaction will, by definition, also be eliminated.

The important thing is that the individual is able to recognize that blocking behaviour is caused by external forces and that it does not mean they have a malign personality. If that were to be implied, then feedback about the behaviour would be threatening and it would be met with strong defensive behaviour. But because these are natural and normal reactions and, given similar circumstances, many people would do the same sort of thing, acknowledging that you do these things does not brand you as a bad manager or a lousy staff member. Presented as a behaviour, not a personality issue, the reaction of individuals is 'Thank goodness. Now I understand why I'm doing these things and what I can or can't do about it.'

5 Identifying what to do differently to improve performance

The next piece of data that is given to Roberta is the list of what she thinks she should consider doing differently in order to improve her performance. The list is limited to the 20 behaviours she thinks are most critical for performance improvement in her job. Interestingly, she is already doing some of these things. (In no instance have we ever come across a case where what an individual thinks they should be doing is completely different from what they are doing. You're always going to be doing a number of things that work well. The question is simply whether there are other things that would work better.)

On the list of 20 things Roberta thinks she ought to consider doing to improve her performance there are half a dozen that are already among her top 20 behaviours – i.e. she is already giving them high priority, (once again, performance-sustaining behaviours are in italics and performance-accelerating behaviours are in plain text):

▪ Stating arguments forcefully.

▪ *Taking things through to completion.*

▪ Confronting difficult decisions.

▪ Helping people to learn from their mistakes.

▪ *Helping people overcome pressures in their jobs.*

▪ *Letting people know how they are being evaluated.*

And there are another 14 things she thinks she should be considering doing to improve her performance, but that she is not focusing on currently:

▪ Look for examples of best practice and reinforce them.

▪ *Work for a win-win resolution to conflicts.*

▪ *Make sure people don't deviate from standard process and procedure.*

■ *Require quality output from everyone.*

■ *Give people a sense of belonging.*

■ *Do things correctly first time, every time.*

■ Keep focused on the big issues facing the business.

■ Make sure people live up to their commitments.

■ *Always do the homework before taking action.*

■ Provide clear direction for people.

■ Always look for the better way to do something.

■ Try to anticipate threats to the business.

■ Ensure that systems and processes add value.

■ Create integrative processes and systems.

This is not a list of 'must do' behaviours. Whether focusing more on these behaviours and less on what she is currently doing will result in improved performance is a subject for consideration and discussion. Some of the things on this list will have a greater impact on performance than others. Roberta needs to decide which. However, the important issue is that these are *her* ideas; she owns them and she can decide whether to accept them or not. The probability of her changing her behaviour in some manner is greatly enhanced by this fact. It's hard not to like your own ideas.

❝it's hard not to like your own ideas❞

It's also very useful for Roberta to have her ideas out on paper. If she wishes to discuss her performance and what she can do to improve it, this can form the agenda for discussion. The bottom line is improved performance.

6 Aligning behavioural changes with organizational objectives

'Ask them', as we've pointed out, is not the same as 'Let them run off and do whatever they feel like'. The objective of doing things differently is to improve performance, but nobody works in a vacuum where what they do has no effect on other people's performance. In any organizational context, change must be led by objectives. Roberta Webb works in the Eastern Europe finance department of her company. What she does affects not just her individual performance but also the performance of her department and the performance of her internal clients. So before she runs off and changes what she is doing it might not be a bad idea to check whether or not her ideas are aligned with the department's objectives.

At this stage the CPI process enlists input from significant others. These people can be the individual's manager, critical co-workers, customers or subordinates. It isn't a 360° feedback process. It's probably best described as a vector feedback process. Getting a whole lot of people with half-baked ideas involved in a discussion of what you should be doing to improve your performance is a waste of time and energy, and it has a reasonable probability of adding unnecessary stress to the situation. A vector approach helps avoid this. The point is to choose who represents the most important and valuable vector. In most cases that is your boss, but in some instances it might be a customer or a close colleague. In Roberta's case it's her boss.

This being so, concurrent with Roberta completing her questionnaire, her boss completed another questionnaire. It asked the boss what he thought the Finance Manager, Eastern Europe, should do to manage her role most effectively. The output was a list of specific behaviours that was then compared with Roberta's lists.

Of the behaviours considered (by Roberta's boss) to be most appropriate for the Finance Manager, Eastern Europe, the following are among the top 20 things she is already currently doing:

- *Take things through to completion.*
- *Break broad targets down into areas where action can be taken.*
- *Simplify complex problems for people.*
- *Always treat people with respect.*
- Confront difficult decisions.

■ *Set and focus on the priorities.*

■ Get people committed to common objectives.

Of the behaviours considered (by Roberta's boss) to be most appropriate for the Finance Manager, Eastern Europe, the following are among the top 20 things she also believes she should be doing:

■ *Work for a win-win resolution to conflicts.*

■ *Always do the homework before taking action.*

■ Provide clear direction for people.

■ Ensure that systems and processes add value.

■ Look for examples of best practice and reinforce them.

■ *Make sure people don't deviate from standard process and procedure.*

And finally, in addition to the above, the following behaviours are considered (by Roberta's boss) to be appropriate for the Finance Manager, Eastern Europe:

■ *Stress the importance of attention to detail.*

■ Give people visible recognition for good work.

■ Help people see how their work dovetails with others.

■ Get people cooperating rather than competing.

■ Move decision levels downward as far as practical.

■ *Always complete jobs on schedule.*

■ Actively solicit suggestions and opinions.

■ *Stand by colleagues.*

■ *Make a careful assessment of risks.*

■ Look at the business from a strategic point of view.

■ *Think problems through logically and precisely.*

What we have here is an agenda for a discussion on performance improvement that is designed to ensure agreement and commitment.

The reason why a discussion centred on this list will end with agreement on a set of behaviour changes is that it *begins* with agreement. The first seven things that Roberta's boss thinks she should be doing are things she *is* doing. Bingo: they're on the same wavelength right away. The next six things the boss thinks she should be doing are also what *she* thinks she should be doing. Bingo again: Roberta and her boss have agreed on two sets of behaviours in a row. The boss thinks her ideas are great and she thinks his are great. From her point of view he's obviously both intelligent and perceptive. So, therefore, when his list has another eleven things on it that she isn't doing currently and hasn't thought about as yet, she is prepared to think they might be worth considering. If Roberta and her boss work through all these ideas they're bound to come up with an agreed set of behaviours that meet both their objectives. This is a clear win-win.

But what if what the boss thinks should be done is completely different from what the subordinate thinks? This would raise some very important issues, not the least of which might be that the subordinate might consider that they are in the wrong job. However, in thousands of instances of using this approach neither we nor any of the consultants with whom we work have ever come across a case where there was not some level of agreement between the two parties. It's this initial agreement that makes the process work time after time.

7 Creating continuous performance improvement

To make performance improvement continuous, go back to step 1 and work through the process again. Do this every three or four months. The process is simple. It takes about an hour of each individual's time and it gets easier and quicker as it's repeated. It creates tremendous energy, enthusiasm, motivation, commitment and success. And nothing succeeds like success. If you don't think you can afford an hour of your time once every three or four months, then you aren't serious about achieving continuous performance improvement. Nothing of worth is achieved without effort.

> **" nothing of worth is achieved without effort "**

Chapter summary

All performance improvement and all organizational change begin with individuals. Because change is generally incremental, effective adaptation to change should be correspondingly incremental. To maintain optimal effectiveness you should continuously adapt your behaviour to the constant small changes taking place in your job. This is the process of continuous performance improvement (CPI). It means you get to the front of the wave and you stay there. In a commercial for American Express, the Chelsea Football Club coach, Jose Mourinho, ascribes his success to always being one step ahead. That's what continuous performance improvement is about.

The process is straightforward:

- Identify your current behaviour – the 20 or so things that you do most to leverage your performance and that drive 80 percent or more of the results you achieve.
- Understand how you make these behaviours visible to others.
- Identify what you are doing that is blocking performance.
- Identify what is causing you to behave this way and deal with the causes.
- Determine what you need to do differently to improve your performance.
- Evaluate these behaviours in terms of the degree to which they align with organizational objectives.
- Go through the process every four to six months – frequently enough to ensure that you stay one step ahead rather than constantly playing catch-up.

Nothing of worth is achieved without effort.

12

Continuous performance improvement on a wider scale

Here, you see, it takes all the running you do can to keep in one place. If you want to get somewhere else, you must run at least twice as fast as that. (The Queen in *Through the Looking Glass*, by Lewis Carroll)

Unfortunately, one of the snares into which managers fall when they are trying to create commitment to performance goals is the TT trap. They assume that people can be presented with a goal and that, with a little persuasion and some enthusiastic cheerleading, they will all commit to it. But as we've all learned the hard way, it doesn't work like that. Committing to a common goal implies behaviour change, and achieving successful behaviour change requires following the principles of Behaviour Kinetics, one of which is to take an AT approach wherever possible. Buy-in is achieved when people feel some ownership of the ideas. The key word here is 'some'. Not every idea has to be your own, but you feel a lot more committed to the team's performance if at least some of your thoughts, efforts and opinions have gone into what it's doing.

CPI in a team

The first step in applying the CPI process to a team is to get each of the team members to identify what they are doing currently and what they think they need to do to improve their own performance. Let's take the team in which Roberta Webb, whom we met in the previous chapter, works. There are nine members of the Eastern European Finance Team. To begin the CPI process, each completed a 'Momentum CPI' questionnaire and went through an individual feedback process similar to Roberta's. They then met to discuss the results and decide how to improve the team's overall performance.

The basic building block for any change is the individual. Creating a high-performance team is like completing a jigsaw puzzle: when you get all the pieces to fit together they create an attractive picture. If you fail to get them to fit together they remain an ugly and untidy pile of pieces. Once each of the members of a team has gone through the CPI steps they have a clear idea of what they need to do individually to drive performance forward. The next thing they need to know is how their goals and behaviours fit with the rest of the team; they have all the pieces and now they have to put them together.

The key to this is mutual accountability. Without it no group can become an effective team. The concept of mutual accountability is fairly simple to describe – one for all and all for one – but not quite so simple to achieve. Katzenbach and Smith comment that 'Our culture emphasizes individual accomplishments and makes us uncomfortable trusting our career aspirations to outcomes dependent on the performance of others'.

In the seventeenth century Thomas Hobbes argued that the natural state of human beings is one of perpetual struggle against one another. Independence is highly valued in Western society. In the USA, 4 July isn't called Group Cooperation Day. The big stumbling block with 'one for all' is that 'one' has to give up a number of things that he or she would rather like to keep. 'All for one' sounds a lot more attractive, but it's only one side of the bargain. The moral philosophers like Hobbes seem to have got it right; self-interest rules behaviour, so mutual accountability is only likely to be accepted when all the parties see it giving them additional benefit.

In Chapter eight we talked about how high-performance teams generate results that far exceed the sum of what each of their individual members could achieve. A good team beats a collection of good individuals every time. The problem is stated pithily by the legendary baseball manager who took the New York Yankees to ten championships and five world series titles, Casey Stengel. His observation was: 'It's easy to get the players; it's getting them to play together that's the hard part'.

❝ a good team beats a collection of good individuals every time ❞

But there is a way to help people to work/play together. If you can establish a common purpose and common goals you can get on with the business of driving continuous performance improvement. The single most important characteristic of effective teams is that every individual in the team feels a deep commitment to a common purpose and common goals.

So the second step in the CPI process is to get all the members of the team into a room to agree a common purpose and a common goal. Nothing progresses further until a stated goal and purpose has been discussed, written down and displayed on a screen or board. Once that's happened the hard question has to be asked of every individual in turn: are you fully committed to the goal or aren't you? Public statements of commitment are required.

Once that's done the team can begin to look in turn at the lists of what each individual is doing and what they think they should be doing differently to improve performance. The criterion applied to each behaviour on these lists is whether it contributes to the achievement of the team's common goal and purpose. If it does, it is endorsed by the team and is guaranteed support; if it doesn't, it gets struck off the list. Team behaviour doesn't change until individual behaviour changes; everyone must be prepared to shoulder their share of the burden.

The next thing to go up on the screen is the list of the team's top 20 behaviours.

Here is the list of the Eastern European Finance Team (performance-accelerating behaviours in plain text and *performance-sustaining behaviours* in italics):

- Accept responsibility for all outcomes, good or poor.
- Review past performance to see what can be learned from it.

- Try to exceed performance expectations.
- Encourage people to find ways to be more effective.
- *Keep a finger on the pulse of what is going on.*

- *Make sure people don't fail because of lack of appropriate resources.*
- *Help people overcome pressures in their jobs.*
- Help people to learn from their mistakes.
- Clear away obstructive processes and procedures.
- Get people to feel involved and enthusiastic about what they do.

- *Help people develop the necessary skills for their jobs.*
- *Give people confidence in themselves.*
- *Break broad targets down into areas where action can be taken.*
- *Simplify complex problems.*
- *Think changes through carefully.*

- *Keep people abreast of changes in systems and processes.*
- Look at the business from a strategic point of view.
- Insist that people give their best effort.
- Ensure that systems and processes add value.
- Get people to take responsibility for their careers.

Just as good bouillabaisse is different from the pure sum of its ingredients, an effective team's behaviour is not the same as a simple aggregation of its members' behaviours. To improve its performance a team has to understand which behaviours it is currently focusing its energy and attention on and then it needs to go through the same process as it did with each of its individual members' behaviours, asking of each specific behaviour whether it contributes to the common goal and purpose of the team or doesn't. Those that add value remain on the list and those that don't get removed.

Then there is the question of what the team is doing to block perfor-mance. Each one of the individuals around the table has confronted this issue in terms of their own behaviour, and now it's the turn of the team as a whole to broach the subject. The same questions are asked of team performance-blocking behaviours as are asked of an individual. What is causing this behaviour? Can we deal with the cause and remove it? If we can't remove the cause (e.g. this is a head office dictum) then what can we do to mitigate our reaction to it? What can we do to lessen the blocking effect it has on our performance? A good discussion of these issues around the table has a major liberating effect on a team.

Once this process has been completed, the next stage is to look at what the team thinks it should be doing differently to improve its perfor-mance. The following is the list of the top 20 behaviours on which the Eastern European Finance Team believes it needs to focus energy and attention in order to improve its performance (the items in bold are things it is already doing):

■ **Insist that people give their best effort**.

■ *Keep a finger on the pulse of what is going on*.

■ **Get people to feel involved and enthusiastic about what they do**.

■ Allow people freedom to deal with things for which they have been given responsibility.

■ Create team spirit.

■ **Encourage people to find ways to be more effective**.

■ *Make sure people don't fail because of lack of appropriate resources*.

■ Do things that make a noticeable difference.

■ *Do things correctly first time, every time*.

■ *Take things through to completion*.

■ Take clear initiative.

- **Review past performance to see what can be learned from it**.

- Assess the long-term outcomes of actions.

- Make sure people live up to their commitments.

- Get people cooperating rather than competing.

- Reward achievement and results rather than effort.

- *Keep people abreast of changes in systems and processes*.

- **Help people to learn from their mistakes**.

- Try to anticipate threats to the business.

- **Ensure that systems and processes add value**.

Once again the team has to go through the process of deciding whether each of these behaviours makes a significant contribution to the achievement of the common goal and purpose. Then, from the remaining list of behaviours, the team needs to select the ten most important and decide how to implement them.

This process is based on the principles of Behaviour Kinetics. It focuses purely on behaviour that is observable and measurable; it is goal specific; it is AT; it provides everyone with clear ownership of the decisions. And because it is based on Behaviour Kinetics it works. Creating a high-performing team is a complex exercise in behaviour change and unless it is approached from a structured and scientifically based (i.e. observable, measurable, predictable, controllable) perspective it does not have a great chance of success. Everyone has been on a number of team-building exercises. They create some change, but they rarely create a high-performance team simply because they don't get past trying to build relationships. They don't ask the hard question: 'Are you willing to work on the basis of one for all and all for one?' Until you get commitment to this you don't get past having a friendly group who enjoy a drink together after work.

Improving the performance of organizations

The many issues of large-scale organizational change are too numerous to be dealt with in this book. If you want to pursue the topic, a good place to start is the books by John Kotter. However, successful change is based on a number of constants. They sit at the heart of Behaviour Kinetics. We've talked about them earlier in the book, but just to refresh your memory, here they are again. They form the basis of a blueprint for change – in individuals, teams, large groups or complete organizations.

Creating heat or light

There are, as we pointed out in Chapters 1 and 2, a number of constants in the continuous performance improvement process. They apply at every level and in every situation. The first constant is the need for people either to feel the heat or see the light. There needs to be a reason for change and it has to be a reason that people feel in their stomachs. From his research John Kotter concludes that 'Changing behaviour is less a matter of giving people analysis to influence their thoughts than helping them to see a truth to *influence their feelings*' (italics his). The first of his eight stages of successful large-scale change is to create a sense of urgency, which he says 'gets people off the couch, out of a bunker, and ready to move'. A sense or urgency creates either heat or light – or sometimes both.

Proceeding one step at a time

The second CPI constant is to proceed one step at a time. Organizational change takes place when individuals change their behaviour and when the teams in which they operate change their behaviour. Momentum is a key word. In any organization about 10–15 percent of the people are consistently receptive to change, about 10–15 percent are steadfastly opposed to change, and the remaining 70–80 percent are undecided and sit of the fence to see what happens. To institute CPI you need to start with the people who are supportive of change and help them demonstrate its success. With each success, you then begin to involve more and more of the undecided. Success is highly attractive. Everyone loves a winner and they all want to be part of the winning process. If you proceed one step at a time, you will attract increasing numbers of the undecided off the fence and into the camp of change support, and you will create an unstoppable momentum for change.

Leave the resistors alone until you have created an unstoppable momentum. If you involve them when the change is in its infancy they will kill it relatively easily. Faced with a clear momentum of change, however, they either come on board or get swept away.

Benchmarking the start point of the change

The third CPI constant is to define the start point for change. You need to establish the level of current performance and to benchmark people's current behaviour. The objective is *continuous* performance improvement, and that can only be achieved if you are able to monitor progress constantly, starting from the first steps. Without tracking based on clear measurement, change becomes random. Unless you track what you are doing against your results, how do you know what caused them? We're constantly bombarded with 'reasons' for things – why the stock market moves, why consumer spending changes, why traffic accidents, street crime, obesity or whatever increase or decrease. But there is rarely a clear link established between a particular 'reason' and the result. Are alcohol and drugs the cause of traffic accidents, or are accidents caused by powerful engines, poor roads, poor driver education or not enough police? Obviously all these things contribute to the result, but unless you can determine the relative effect of each how can you establish priorities and focus attention on dealing with the problem?

❝ without tracking based on clear measurement, change becomes random ❞

The CPI process establishes the start point at every level, beginning with the individual. Just as you can determine what an individual is doing and what a team is doing, you can ascertain the dominant behaviour of a business unit. Here, for instance, are the dominant behaviours of the Eastern European Division of Roberta's company. Broken down into the following four categories they provide a pretty clear picture of the culture of the division. It's one that is results-focused, creates an exciting and challenging place to work, is supportive of its people, and uses systems and processes to coordinate and integrate activities and outputs.

■ Creating challenge and excitement:

- getting people to feel involved and enthusiastic about what they do;

- getting people excited about challenges;

- encouraging people to find ways to be more effective.

■ Focusing on results:

- focusing on the priorities;

- accepting responsibility for all outcomes;

- always meeting commitments;

- keeping a finger on the pulse of what is going on;

- doing things that make a noticeable difference.

■ Supporting people:

- giving people confidence in themselves;

- standing by colleagues;

- helping people overcome pressures in their jobs;

- helping people to learn from their mistakes;

- making sure people don't fail because of lack of appropriate resources;

- actively soliciting suggestions and opinions.

■ Process and integration:

- creating integrative processes and systems;

- looking at the business from a strategic point of view;

- ensuring that systems and processes add value;

- working to longer-term goals;

- clearing away obstructive processes and procedures;

- reviewing past performance to see what can be learned from it.

If the Eastern European Division wants to change the way it operates, it now has a solid benchmark from which to start. If it acquires a competitor, it knows the sorts of behaviours it needs to reinforce within the acquired company to bring its culture into line with its own.

Focusing on observable behaviour

The fourth constant in the CPI process is to make sure you maintain a focus on observable behaviour. Behaviour determines performance. It's what people *do* that makes a difference. The more clearly you can identify people's specific behaviour and link it to measurable results, the easier it is to improve performance.

There are two elements to this process. For the first part of the behaviour–performance link, it's necessary to focus purely on behaviour that can be observed and measured. If you can't see it being done then you can't be sure about it. Intent and action are two very different things. Remarks like 'People know that I want them to be prepared to take considered risks' don't describe behaviour, they describe intent. Where was the behaviour that communicated the message? People only 'know' when they have understood a message. Telling them that they need to be prepared to take considered risks is an initial step in the process, but there needs to be clear observable behaviour that reinforces and supports the message.

In the Eastern European Division of the company we've been using as an example, if it believes that 'getting people involved and enthusiastic about what they do' is important to drive performance, then it needs to determine how it actually goes about doing this. Is it a matter of quarterly pep rallies? Is it a matter of linking the reward structure to achievement? Is it about reinforcing good performance, about providing feedback and support, or about making sure that people actually make contributions to discussions and decisions? Whatever it decides, it needs to translate into observable behaviour. We find it easier to believe what we see than what we just hear about.

> **we find it easier to believe what we see than what we just hear about**

And measurement of the second part of the behaviour–performance link, the performance, is equally important. If the desired performance output is improved profit and increased market share, we need to able to measure these things and track the changes.

Guiding change, not directing it

The final constant is the necessity to maintain an AT approach to performance improvement. The results of AT are all positive – involvement, ownership, commitment, a sense of worth and achievement, motivation, energy, enthusiasm and superior performance. The evidence is there for all to see. It's called Toyota.

Chapter summary

Continuous performance improvement requires an investment of time and effort, a lot of it up front. It also requires tenacity. Continuous *means* continuous. It's not a process that can be switched on once and expected to run without further effort or intervention.

The process is essentially the same whether it be applied to an individual, to a team, a group of some kind, or an entire organization. The first prerequisite is a clear sense of a performance goal. Without strong commitment to achieving a goal, behaviour change never takes place, no matter what the level or scale. And goals that drive change either involve seeing the light – i.e. seeing the potential and value of improving performance – or feeling the heat, meaning that the current situation is becoming increasingly uncomfortable and untenable and will continue to do so unless some change takes place. We would all like to believe that people respond to the logic of the need for change, but the fact is they seldom do. Change is driven much more by emotion than logic.

At an individual level, when people decide what they need to do to improve their performance it's relatively simple to link these ideas with the objectives of their boss or their business unit. At the team level, the process gets a bit more complicated and requires more emphasis. The whole idea behind getting people to agree to things in front of their close colleagues is that it makes turning their back on their commitment much harder. If you promise yourself you will stop smoking but you don't tell anyone, you have only yourself to make you feel guilty if you continue to smoke. If you promise six or eight of your colleagues you will quit and you don't, it's a great deal more uncomfortable to face them. This concept holds true for change at all organizational levels. Commitments need to be made openly and in the knowledge that they will be observed and monitored.

The process of continuous performance improvement is based on the principles of Behaviour Kinetics and there is a series of steps that need to be borne in mind. Change is a stepwise process. You start at the beginning (what you're doing now) and you proceed one step at a time towards reaching a change goal. If you want to run a marathon you start with your current level of fitness and you work every day on getting fitter and running a bit further. You build up until one day you run the 26 miles and you've achieved your goal. You track your progress in a way that is measurable and observable. The key is to focus on behaviour and to make sure it's observable and measurable.

Continuous performance improvement is not difficult to achieve. It requires tenacity and focus. The steps have been outlined pretty clearly in this book. If you follow them you will improve performance. If you don't, you've just reduced the probability of performance improvement. Nothing of value is achieved without effort.

2

Behaviour Kinetics approaches to performance improvement

Part 2 provides examples of several different approaches to the application of Behaviour Kinetics. In each instance a behavioural technology and methodology is applied to the situation. As we've emphazied earlier, people need help to answer the questions 'What are you doing currently and what should you be doing differently to improve your performance?' The degree to which a behavioural technology helps to obtain clear answers to these questions determines to a large extent how focused change becomes. Not all change improves performance. In most change efforts large amounts of time, energy and resources are wasted going down blind alleys. Performance improvement requires clear and intense focus.

The following four case studies show how measurable change has been introduced in a variety of situations with diverse goals and objectives. In each case a different diagnostic approach has been used. Catalyst UK has used its i-Scope questionnaire to create measurable change in a durable goods manufacturer. Dr David West has used his company's set of sales behaviour instruments, the Sales Behaviour Diagnosis, to improve the performance and profit of a key account team of an IT business solutions company. Chris Dunn and Andy Pellant of AdviserPlus have used a behaviour profiling approach to determine the fit of behaviour to a specific role/job at Snap-On Tools. Professor Rick Roskin has used his management behaviour diagnostic Mach One to create change in a large food processing company.

More than one road leads to Rome, but not *all* roads lead there. There are a number of ways of identifying the behaviour required to perform a job most effectively. If organizations are serious about improving the performance of their people, they need to get serious about the identification and measurement of *observable behaviour*. Personality profiling has helped people and organizations gain an understanding of differences, which helps facilitate interpersonal relationships. But personality doesn't predict behaviour well at all, and different jobs, to be done well, require different behaviours. Competency frameworks have moved things significantly forward, but they are general in nature, covering a range of functions or jobs. Now the next step needs to be taken – to identify the *specific* behaviours that are necessary to perform a *specific* job most effectively, to measure the current behaviours of the incumbents of those jobs, and to elicit their ideas and suggestions for performance improvement.

13

It ain't what you do, it's the way that you do it

Kevin Howes and Mark Reynolds
Catalyst People Ltd

Catalyst is a consultancy dedicated to performance management. Its focus is on what it terms the 'Behaviour drives performance' equation, and its approach is based on the principles of Behaviour Kinetics. Its methodology is driven by two audits: first, the validation of the strategy and, second, the capability of the people to deliver that strategy. Its work on the latter is based on data gleaned from two complementary behavioural profiling tools – i-Scope and Momentum CPI – both of which identify the observable and measurable behaviour of individuals and teams. Catalyst has successfully applied a Behaviour Kinetics approach in its work with clients like DaimlerChrysler, Accident Exchange, England Rugby, Oracle, Virgin Atlantic and Epson. The case study below is an example of its work, using the behavioural diagnostic tool i-Scope.

In today's business world speed is everything. The pace of change and the unrelenting advance of technology have combined to create an environment where those who execute and implement with accuracy and speed take the spoils, while those who choose to ruminate, procrastinate and eventually respond are most frequently penalized and punished.

How many times have you heard the conversation about a failed business initiative that includes the lament, 'It wasn't so much what we did – but the way that we did it'? A mediocre strategy or plan effectively executed more often than not will win over a brilliant strategy dragged down by poor implementation. All too frequently, meetings end with that wonderful feeling of satisfaction having reviewed all the data, listened to the ideas and opinions before uniting around a powerful action plan – only to find a short time later that the on-the-ground implementation didn't quite match the time and energy investment of the strategy. The acid test is not what people say they will or must do: it's what they *actually* do that really makes the difference.

A brief introduction to i-Scope

i-Scope measures behaviour along four basic dimensions:

- *Drive* – focused on creating momentum, movement and action in otherwise static environments. Drive is an essential entrepreneurial behaviour for change.

- *Future orientation* – the degree to which individuals think about, evaluate and assess where the business is going and where it should be going. It is about longer-term strategic thinking and action.

- *Results orientation* – examines whether people convert ideas into achievable goals and then work towards the achievement of these goals. It is about shorter-term tactical thinking and action.

- *Managing style* – behaviour that gets people aligned to organizational strategy, direction and goals and involves them in the implementation and achievement of these goals

These dimensions are referred to as 'muscle groups'. They break down into specific sets of behaviours that can be observed and measured. Identification of observable and measurable behaviours is a prerequisite of any Behaviour Kinetics application. Each dimension (muscle group) can be developed through use and application or can, through lack of attention, have less and less effect on performance. i-Scope generates data that reflect what individuals see themselves currently doing and what they think they need to be doing to meet the demands of the situation. On the basis of this information they can therefore take action to exercise whichever muscle group is most appropriate.

The behaviours associated with the 'Drive' group are:

- ▦ *Initiating* – the things that people do that exhibit self-driven initiative and enterprise. These are the things that people do spontaneously and without instruction.

- ▦ *Load bearing* – the full acceptance of responsibility for outcomes, without dodging or ducking. These behaviours reflect the view that 'the buck stops here'.

- ▦ *Plate spinning* – the ability to balance conflicting priorities, often between urgent and pressing short-term demands and longer-term strategic objectives.

The behaviours associated with 'Future orientation' are broken down into:

- ▦ *Adapting* – behaviours that demonstrate the ability to adapt and flex what an individual does to deal with uncertainty and ambiguity.

- ▦ *Exploring opportunities* – actions involved with seeking out opportunity and exploiting it.

- ▦ *Innovating* – behaviours that take a new approach to achieving objectives and solving problems.

- ▦ *Visioning* – behaviours break down a strategic vision into manageable parts that people can understand and implement.

The behaviours associated with 'Results orientation' are grouped into:

- ▦ *Risk spotting* – the identification and assessment of risks to the business.

- ▦ *Risk insuring* – behaviours focused on developing contingency plans to cope with risk situations.

- ▦ *Path clearing* – behaviours that deal with removing obstacles to achievement.

And the behaviours associated with 'Managing style' – aligning individual behaviour with organizational objectives – are broken down into:

- *Directing* – making decisions without consultation or reference to others.

- *Collaborating* – seeking input, ideas and information from others and incorporating them in decision making.

Figure 13.1 shows a sample i-Scope profile of a group of directors. The behaviour demonstrated by this profile is 'decide and do'. It is highly action-oriented. It shows a number of high 'initiating behaviours' – self-driven initiative and enterprise, and high load-bearing behaviour, with the acceptance of responsibility for outcomes. This is out-front, striving, driving, high-energy, swashbuckling behaviour. It gets things done, come hell or high water.

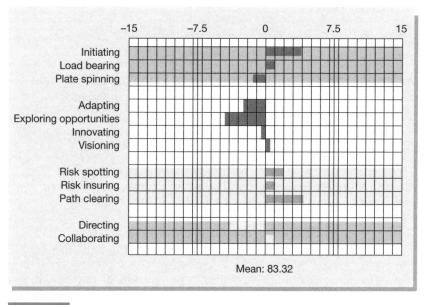

Figure 13.1 i-Scope profile of a group of directors

However, there are some danger signals. The profile shows few behaviours that focus on finding or developing new ways to do things or new approaches to problems. The preference is for repeating what has worked before. This type of behaviour gets lots of things done quickly, but because no effort is made to operationalize strategy and translate it into clear and discrete actions and objectives it is unclear what is important and what is needed to drive the strategy forward, as opposed to what is unimportant and a waste of time and resources. Added to that is a lack of managerial flexibility, as evidenced by the low level of adapting behaviours.

❝ all things only remain equal in theoretical economic models ❞

For the senior management of a company in a changing and changeable industry, this is a high-risk behavioural profile. It assumes that what they are doing now is correct – that they are focused on the right issues, dealing with the right problems, and heading in the right direction. It also assumes that the environment is not going to change. It's an 'all things being equal' strategy, and unfortunately all things only remain equal in theoretical economic models.

Helping a company regain its entrepreneurial edge

In early 2004 Catalyst was asked by the directors of a durable goods manufacturer, with a reputation for creativity, innovation and customer focus, to work with it on the implementation of a new corporate strategy. The company had begun to experience falling revenues and shrinking margins, and competitors were beginning to eat into its market share. The industry was also changing rapidly, largely due to two factors: increased disposable income across the economy and changing consumer tastes. It had become increasingly clear that a new approach to the business was needed.

The first step involved a meeting with the chief executive of the company to discuss and decide how to help the top team identify the issues around gaining commitment to the new corporate strategy. The strategy called for a number of people to make significant changes in the way they managed their jobs. It also involved a number of structural changes. Catalyst was asked to help people, beginning with the directors of the company, to work through and commit to the appropriate changes of behaviour.

Catalyst began the process by asking the directors to complete the behavioural diagnostic, i-Scope. For a business to have the best chance of delivering its strategy successfully, the right balance of behaviours is required, and of course that balance varies depending upon the situation, needs and priorities of the business.

When all the directors had completed the i-Scope diagnostic, one-to-one meetings were arranged with each of them to feed back and discuss their results. Without exception, the directors demonstrated high energy and a strong results focus, combined with a short-term orientation. The behaviour described a team that was focused on clear objectives and on delivering results in a tight time frame, but that spent little time exploring new opportunities, new ways of working, or finding solutions to long-standing problems. It also showed that they spent little time or effort in soliciting ideas from people, or listening and learning from them.

The team had been recruited for its creativity, flair and innovation, but it had become bogged down with short-term priorities and actions. At the time of the Catalyst intervention, over 40 initiatives and projects were running in the company. The scramble for resources was frantic and few of the initiatives' objectives were being achieved. The directors acknowledged that the best description of the situation was that it was about fighting alligators rather than draining the swamp.

Processing the information

The results of the i-Scope diagnosis showed that, in almost every case, the current behaviour of each of the directors represented a significant change from how they had managed in the past. The pressures and demands of their new roles were quite evidently causing a high degree of stress as they struggled to discover effective ways to deal with the situation. Their initiating behaviours were down; innovating behaviours were down; and path-clearing behaviours were dramatically increased. Drive and creativity had given way to struggling to hack a way through a tangle of problems and obstacles that continued to crop up. To change the metaphor, they appeared to be in a constant fire-fighting mode.

In addition, their behaviours showed a much stronger focus on risk spotting and risk insuring – trying to identify where fires were going to crop up and working on contingency plans to deal with them. While contingency planning is essential in a changing business, it is best done in the context of a clear strategy and clear goals and objectives. In a short-term fire-fighting context, attempts at contingency planning tend to descend into confusion and chaos under the pressure of many conflicting demands.

When the directors met to review the data, they recognized they did not have a clear set of goals and objectives to which they were all committed. The changes in the industry, in the marketplace and in the company had taken them by surprise and left them in semi-limbo between their old (highly successful) organizational systems and management style and a completely new approach to the business. There was no lack of will to succeed or to change. The problem was how to change and to what?

Looking at the needs of the business, the directors developed the following pictures of how they had approached issues in the past and how they were currently behaving. The results are summarized in Figures 13.2 and 13.3.

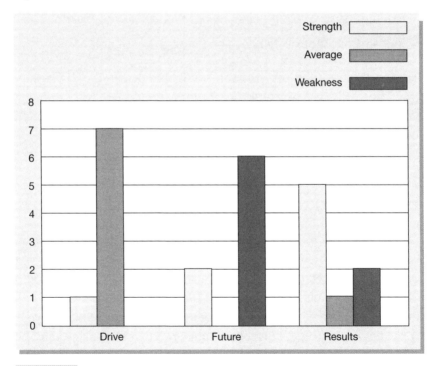

Figure 13.2 Current i-Scope profile

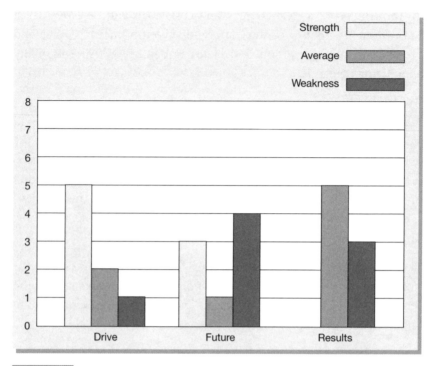

Figure 13.3 Former i-Scope profile

The results show that the welter of conflicting demands and constant problems had sapped the directors of a lot of their drive and energy and taken their eye off the future. The fire-fighting issues of the present dominated their behaviour. The balance had been tipped heavily toward delivering day-to-day results and away from a view of where the business and the industry were heading.

Team discussion and decisions

As discussed in a number of the earlier chapters in this book, change begins when individuals and groups understand what they are doing currently and when they begin to look at what is working for them and what is not working. If this process is followed by getting them to think through what they should do differently, a momentum for change is created. A key concept of Behaviour Kinetics is that individuals must be able to make their own decisions for change on the basis of what they are currently doing and what the situation requires of them. The one thing that must be avoided at all costs is evaluative comment from outsiders – i.e. imposing values of good or bad on the behaviour of others. There is no question that some behaviour is positive and creates momentum and that some is negative and blocks momentum, but it is important to remember (a) that it is *behaviour*, and (b) that the behaviour is basically the result of the demands of the situation the individual is facing. Once they understand these two things, people quite readily accept both the positive and negative things they are doing and begin to work out how to change them.

> **❝ change begins when individuals and groups understand what they are doing currently ❞**

When the directors met to discuss their i-Scope results, the following were some of the comments and observations that were made:

- Our vision:

  - We are giving out confusing messages.

  - We are not clear about what we are here to do.

  - There is no unity of vision.

  - There is a lack of commercial focus.

  - We are a fragile business.

- Our team:

  - Are we a team? Should we be? I keep an open mind about it.

  - The team is too big.

  - There is a CEO team, when the CEO team is together.

  - This is an egalitarian company – decisions can get overturned too easily.

- Our people:

  - The company has outgrown some people.

  - There is no career planning.

  - We do not have good management with a broader view of the business.

- We are an international company with little international experience.

- Confronting non-performance is an issue across the business.

- Too many of our staff don't tell the truth or don't say anything.

■ Our results:

- We have more ideas than resources.

- New ideas seem more important than implementation.

- Some things just don't move forward.

- We have no programme management techniques.

- Cross-functional projects just don't run on time.

- What we have started is not working, yet we keep on starting more.

- I overcompensate for the problems I see.

- We are trying to make everything a project – it dissipates accountability.

Once the directors were able to air these views and get agreement on a number of key issues, the process rapidly switched to dealing with them. They re-examined their proposed strategy and agreed its final form. They set out clear and measurable goals and objectives for each sector of the business. They developed an accepted framework for decision making. And they agreed a process of behaviour feedback among themselves to ensure openness and to reinforce the behaviours necessary to implement the strategy successfully. Then, having got all their ducks in a row, they began to cascade the process down through the organization, maintaining an 'ask them' approach and using i-Scope to help individuals and groups identify their behaviour and assess its effectiveness.

14

Sales behaviour and customer expectation

Dr David West
Director of Learning, The Working Manager Ltd

Dr David West has focused attention on helping sales people improve their sales performance by adapting their behaviours to fit each specific customer/client situation. He has developed a diagnostic instrument, the Sales Behaviour Diagnosis, which identifies and measures (a) the behaviours of sales people, and (b) the behavioural expectations and values of customers. The resultant outputs show the degree to which a salesperson's or sales team's behaviour matches what the customer expects and will respond to most positively. Dr West's approach to behaviour change applies the principles of Behaviour Kinetics. It enables individuals to identify and accept what they are doing currently, to recognize what they should be doing to match customer needs and expectations, to measure the gaps between these two sets of behaviour, to give ownership of the changes to the individuals involved, and to decide step by step how to address the issue and improve performance.

One area in which Behaviour Kinetics is most important and should be most obvious is sales. A lot of work has been done on personality and sales success, but while this may be interesting and valuable from a recruitment point of view, its usefulness is ultimately limited. What the salesperson needs to know is how to adapt to different customers. Put baldly, personality is what we *are* while behaviour is what we *do*. We can change what we do, but not what we are.

The objective of sales training is to get people to do things differently. Therefore it is a little odd that sales trainers use so many personality-based tests in training. If the word 'personality' means anything, it refers to some deeply based, enduring and unchangeable fact or factors about a person – *what you are*. Thus, if you learn that you are, to use Myers-Briggs terminology, an ISTJ while the situation calls for ENFP, you have a problem. There is nothing you can do to change what you are. And if there is nothing you can do to change the situation, then there is – to put no finer point on it – nothing you can do!

While understanding a person's personality may he helpful in knowing how best to deal with them, unless they go around wearing a badge that tells everyone their personality type, or unless you can get them to complete a test there and then, the chances of you knowing what they are, are slight. However, you can see what they *do* and, as Chapter 7 on motivation suggests, you may therefore be able to use their behaviour to infer their personality, if that's what you feel you need to understand.

In selling, it is very important for the salesperson to be able rapidly to identify the needs and drivers of the person to whom they are selling. Having done that, they need to be able to adjust their behaviour to respond to these needs and drivers. This is the key. If sales training is about getting people to do things differently, then it is behaviour that matters – *what you do* as opposed to *what you are*. But sales situations differ, customers differ, customer needs and expectations differ. So sales training needs to be focused on showing people what to do in various situations. Most people can behave in ways, even highly atypical of them, for short periods of time.

Behaviour and values

The way we behave exhibits values, beliefs and priorities, and dictates how people respond to us. The ability to adapt sales behaviours to a variety of different sales situations is a key to successful selling. Customers respond positively to behaviour that shows the salesperson understands the customers' values, beliefs and priorities. We like people who, to use John Wayne's line in *True Grit*, 'remind me of me' and we are less comfortable with people who operate on a different wavelength from us. This has been demonstrated time and time again in sales training sessions.

> **❝ customers respond positively to behaviour that shows the salesperson understands the customers' values ❞**

Oddly enough, most sales training gets behavioural management wrong. The importance of behaviours in selling is not about trying to change the customer's behaviour – as with NLP or operant conditioning – but about changing our, the seller's, behaviour. Not only is this far more likely to work, but in matching our sales behaviour to customers' values we put customers first.

For example, customers may value attention, personalized service and quality. In this type of situation, sales behaviours that focus almost entirely on emphasizing the benefits of a product are unlikely to be successful. However, the customer may start to see the salesperson as someone who shares their values if the salesperson shows behaviours like:

- Being systematic, checking to avoid mistakes and risks.

- Being thorough and careful and paying attention to detail.

- Acting with integrity.

- Documenting what the customer says and ensuring proper answers.

The two of them appear to be on the same wavelength and the customer is far more likely to want to do business with the salesperson.

Another customer may believe that service should be taken for granted and may principally be concerned about what the salesperson can do to help solve some of the problems in their business. The appropriate behaviours in this type of situation may include:

- Investing time to understand the underlying nature of the customer's business.

- Researching problems or opportunities of which the customer may not be aware.

■ Actively encouraging customers to talk about their business issues.

■ Analyzing the customer's business processes.

Think for a moment about the buyers in the big supermarket companies. What sort of people are they likely to be? Well, they are likely to be graduates, possibly in a mathematically related discipline – highly trained and intelligent. What are their criteria for buying? They most probably centre upon returns. Even very large supermarkets have a limit to their square footage and a key criterion is going to be return on shelf space. What behaviour would you think that an intelligent, highly trained, numerate buyer, with return on shelf space on their mind, will react to best? It is highly unlikely to be a sales approach emphasizing 'we are the best' types of behaviours.

The buyer knows that most products are commodities, whether you are talking about mayonnaise, soups or window-cleaning liquids. What the buyer needs to know is whether the demand pattern for your products has been changed by advertising, product-support activities or special offers. They want to know how stocking your product will help increase the supermarket's net revenue – i.e. help solve the perennial problem of narrow profit margins. The buyer wants this information in a calm, analytical manner, with charts and data from test marketing that show understanding of the criteria.

Measurement

Sales behaviour can be measured. And so can customers' values and expectations. Such measurement shows where the behaviour is congruent with what the customer values and where it isn't. We often see sales people behaving in a way that is poles apart from what their customers value. For example, perhaps the customer values personal help, time spent to understand personal and business needs, creatively researching solutions to problems and seeking opportunities – and the salesperson, oblivious to these needs, continues offering the latest off-the-shelf product in a technical and impersonal way.

Sales behaviour can be at cross-purposes with customer values. For example, a customer may indicate that they are ready to respond to serious-minded, creative and scientific behaviour, may want to hear about precise specifications and guarantees of reliability, and may not mind spending a considerable amount of time in this discussion. They may not be interested in trying to establish any kind of personal rapport with the salesperson. 'Give me the facts, just the facts.' However, on the other side of the transaction, the salesperson's behaviour may be a reflection of what they have been trained to do – to try to make sales quickly, to get to the 'close', to emphasize assumed product advantages if possible, and if that doesn't appear to be working to switch to trying to establish a personal rapport with the customer.

The ability to read the behavioural cues – the behavioural preferences or values of the customer – provides a major sales edge. Identifying what matters to a customer and then adapting sales behaviour to reflect these values will help a salesperson to be successful. So, you can use behavioural profiles to improve sales results, whereas you cannot use personality profiles.

A case study

The approach described here has been used with many sales teams, some very large and some smaller. I have chosen a smaller example to make the data more accessible. The company will, of course, remain anonymous.

The sales team concerned is a key account team. In fact, it has only one customer, a major banking institution, which buys hardware and software from the sales team. This customer operates in Europe and the USA. The sales team was concerned that while its sales to the customer were satisfactory, they did not seem to reach the heights that it expected. The team felt, without being able to put their finger on it, that their relationships with the customer, while cordial, were not perfect. The customer did not seem, on many occasions, to respond to the team in the way that it wished it to.

The behavioural model used is known as the Sales Behaviour Diagnosis, as shown in Figure 14.1.

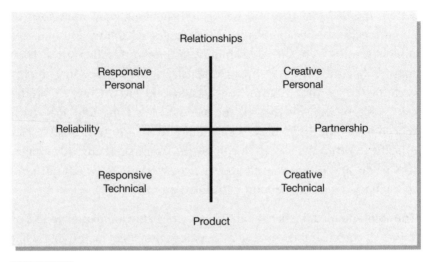

Figure 14.1   The Sales Behaviour Diagnosis model

The first scale, from 'reliability' to 'partnership' is essentially a range from responsive behaviours to creative behaviours. Higher scores on the responsive side indicate behaviours concerned with maintaining quality of delivery. They are behaviours that enable people to perform well in terms of service and in maintaining the integrity of the product or service. Higher scores on the creative side indicate behaviours oriented towards actively looking for new problems and opportunities with customers. They are behaviours centred on attempting to understand how customers' businesses work and how products or services can be used in an innovative and value-adding manner.

The other scale, from 'relationships' to 'product' is essentially a range from personally oriented behaviours to technically oriented behaviours. High scores on the personal side are associated with an interest in people and indicate behaviours directed towards getting to know people as a way of developing business. People who score high in this area exhibit values concerning their relationship with customers, viewing business as a social web. Higher scores on the technical side indicate behaviours oriented towards products or services. People who score high in this area tend to exhibit interactions with customers only at a formal level, viewing business more as a series of opportunities for applying their products or services to customers' organizations.

The team's sales behaviours

Using the Sales Behaviour Diagnostic – a behavioural questionnaire that identifies and measures a range of sales behaviours – the behaviour of the sales team in question was plotted. The results are shown in Figure 14.2. The team's sales behaviours are weighted towards using the establishment of relationships with customers as a principal sales technique rather than using an emphasis on product differentiation and benefits.

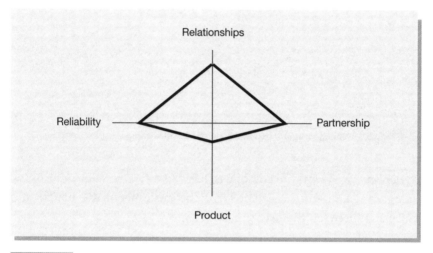

Figure 14.2   The sales team's behaviour pattern

Customer values

However, the effectiveness of a sales team is not a result of their behaviours alone. The key to sales success is whether the team's behaviours match the customers' values and behavioural expectations. All customers have a preference for how they wish to be approached by sales people. As the Sales Behaviour Diagnosis model indicates, some want a quick pitch that identifies the product's advantages and benefits, some want to feel comfortable on the issue of reliability and trust, some want to be able to establish a rapport and relationship with the salesperson, and some want the selling team to become involved – almost as partners – in the solution of the customer's problems.

Figure 14.3 shows what the customer in this example expected in terms of sales behaviour from the sales team. In some sense it reflects the customer's values.

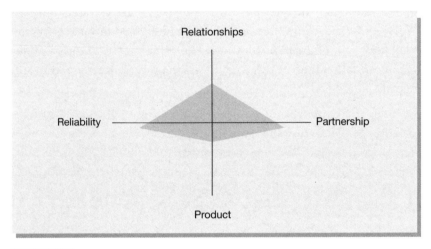

Figure 14.3   The customer's expectations of the sales team

When the two charts are combined (Figure 14.4) – the behaviour of the sales team and the expectations of the customer – the match and mismatch between the two is made clear.

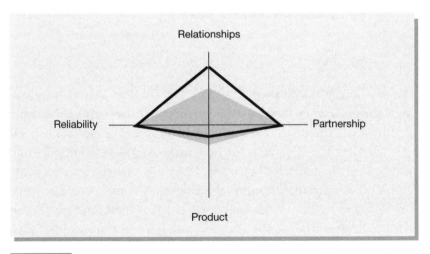

Figure 14.4   The match between the sales team's behaviour and the customer's expectations

A behaviour mismatch

The sales team in this instance was far from being unsuccessful. It can be seen that while there was a fair degree of match between sales behaviours and customer values and expectations, the sales team was clearly exhibiting more relationships behaviours than the customer valued or expected.

So-called relationships behaviours, in brief, are those that aim at giving personal service, looking after the individual customer representative, putting their interests first, developing one-to-one relationships, creating personal trust and close bonds, and working for the customer. The data indicated that the customer did not particularly value such behaviours. This accounted for the fact that the team felt to some extent unhappy about its relationship with the customer's people as individuals, feeling that they were a little 'cold and unfriendly'.

In fact, the customer's values profile is what the Sales Behaviour Diagnosis model calls 'cool professional'. Such customer values can be described in the following behavioural terms:

- Avoidance of errors has a very high priority.
- Avoidance of risk is really important.
- It is very important that suppliers get it right – first time, every time.
- Consistency of delivery matters more than product claims.
- Suppliers are only dropped when things really go wrong.
- Required specifications are made clear to suppliers.
- Suppliers who really research how they can help the business are preferred.
- Special supplier skills and knowledge are more important than product range.
- Internal customers are reasonably expert and expect to be treated that way.
- Requirements are for specialized rather than standardized products.

- Preference is given to suppliers who are primarily problem solvers.

- Suppliers are expected to demonstrate creativity.

It is clear that the behaviours that this customer values do not include a lot of relationships behaviours. Customers like this tend to respond more favourably to behaviours such as:

- Analysing the customer's processes.

- Researching problems or opportunities even when the customer is not aware of them.

- Analyzing customer's business strength and weaknesses.

- Investing time to understand the underlying nature of the customer's business.

- Keeping up to date with changes in the customer's business and organization.

- Spending time discussing overall business issues with customers.

- Being thorough and careful and paying attention to detail.

- Carefully maintaining a reputation for integrity.

- Being systematic, and checking to avoid mistakes and risks.

- Explaining procedures and being thorough in documentation.

- Demonstrating honesty and reliability.

- Never compromising on technical or quality standards.

Averages and individual behaviour profiles

Averages hide differences. The previous charts show the average behaviours of the sales team and the average behavioural expectations and values of the customer group. In Figure 14.5, the sales style of each of the individuals in the sales team are plotted in the form of a scattergram, reducing profiles to a single plot but allowing the team to see the range of their individual behaviours.

Figure 14.6 shows the sales style of the individuals in the sales team compared to the expectations of the individuals in the customer buying

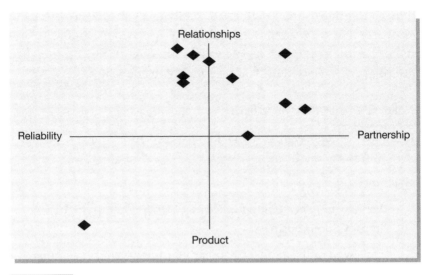

Figure 14.5   The sales styles of each individual in the sales team

group. The diamonds are plots of individuals in the sales team and the circles are plots of individuals within the customer group.

Figure 14.6 makes it clear that what was happening in this situation was that the sales people were using far more relationships behaviour than any of the customer group valued or expected. The resultant discussion

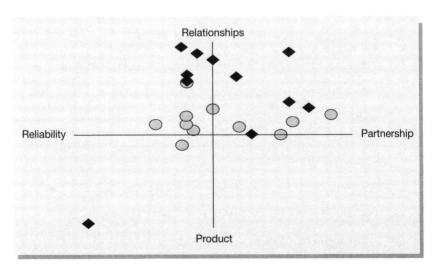

Figure 14.6   A comparison of sales styles and customer expectations

thus concentrated upon getting the individuals in the sales team to recognize that they should underplay such behaviours, and to understand that the customer's people were, rather than being 'unfriendly', just not very interested in creating personal relationships.

What did the customer value?

The most common values (behavioural expectations) of the customer were seen to be as follows:

- Partnership:
  - Your customers are often unaware of what you can do to improve their business.
  - Once you understand a customer's business, you can genuinely and visibly add value to it.
  - It takes some time to understand your customers' business before you can really help them.
  - Virtually every assignment you undertake or every order you get is different.

- Product:
  - You must compete very actively on price.

- Relationships:
  - Your company sells largely to major accounts.
  - In this market, the saying 'People buy people' is very true.
  - Your company must invest in personal support to its customers.

- Reliability:
  - Most changes that you make should be to improve quality and customer service.
  - Your competition is known not to be very efficient.
  - Avoidance of risk is really important in this business.
  - Part of your competitive edge must be in standardizing your service to increase reliability and reduce costs.

- You should concentrate on always having available what your customers want.

What was the sales team doing?

The sales people were most commonly exhibiting the following behaviours:

■ Partnership:

- If a customer wants something non-standard that we do not provide, I seek to understand what business result they want.

- If I lose a customer to a competitor I discuss the decision openly with the customer, seeking to learn from the experience.

- With major customers I seek to understand their critical business issues.

- I produce good proposals because I solve business problems.

- I create new business from existing customers by looking around their company for problems and opportunities they have not seen.

- If it becomes clear that a customer's needs are not within our capabilities I bring in other suppliers and manage a joint proposal for the customer.

- When making the first call on a customer I seek to understand how their business works.

- Customers buy from me again because I make creative recommendations to improve their business.

■ Relationships:

- In preparing proposals I listen attentively to what the customer says.

- When meeting a potential customer for the first time, I try to establish personal rapport and understanding.

- I overcome difficult situations because I relate well and openly with people.

- My most important objective to accomplish with any customer is to establish an ongoing personal, working relationship.

- With all customers I seek to develop mutual trust and respect.

- I measure my success by increasing customers' trust in me as a person.

- I am successful in sales because I constantly enhance the relationships I build up.

- When under competitive pressure I seek the assistance of people in the customer's organization with whom I have developed excellent relationships.

- Customers buy from me because I work hard to get customers to know and trust me.

By getting the sales team to identify and accept their current sales behaviours and to recognize the mismatch between their behaviour and their customers' values and expectations, the sales people were able to decide how to adapt their behaviour to improve their performance. They were able to acknowledge (to a large degree because the data came from what they said about themselves and hence because they felt ownership of the information) that they needed to reduce their emphasis on relationships building. On the basis of the behaviour feedback, they were able to determine which specific relationships behaviours to avoid or modify. In addition, they were able to develop a set of alternative behaviours that allowed them to match the customer's values and expectations more closely, plus being able to decide precisely when and how to use these behaviours.

Ownership of change

The Behaviour Kinetics principle of ensuring that the individuals involved in change have ownership of it is critical in this type of situation. For a variety of reasons people tend to be highly resistant to the ideas and suggestions of others. Sales people in particular have a strong (and understandable) tendency to focus on what has worked for them in the

> **❝ people tend to be highly resistant to the ideas and suggestions of others ❞**

past. 'Experienced' sales people command a greater market value than new and untried ones and they wear their badge of experience proudly. They know what works. However, as the great Harvard professor Fritz Roethlisberger used to say, 'It isn't what you know that gets you into trouble, it's what you know that isn't so'.

People tend to cling to belief in things that 'aren't so' because in their previous experience they *have* been so. What they fail to recognize is that the situation has changed and their former experiences no longer apply. But don't try to tell them that because they won't accept your suggestions. You haven't had their experience; you don't know what they know; they didn't get to where they are today by listening to what uninformed people had to say; etc. We all like our own ideas and suggestions more than we like the ideas and suggestions of others. Ownership is key.

Another example – overcoming the barriers to cross-selling

For a number of years, one of the major clients of a large property company had bought property management services from the company. However, the company had never been able to get any property *sales* business from the client. Sales revenues are much more profitable than service revenues and therefore the case for cross-selling to an established client was highly attractive. But try as they might, all efforts by the property sales team to get an introduction to the client were rebuffed by the property services team. The latter saw the selling agents as brash, shallow people with a short-term focus, and, more importantly, as people who might damage its relationship with their client.

A Sales Behaviour Diagnosis of both the property management team and the property sales team, as well as of the values and expectations of the client, revealed that the property management team was probably quite right in keeping the property sales team at a distance. The property sales team's behaviour was very heavily focused on emphasizing how they were better than their competitors in terms of the prices they could get for properties, the speed with which they could make sales, and the lower costs that they charged clients. Its focus was on a slick sales 'pitch' emphasizing benefits. It devoted little energy or attention to building a relationship with the client – it made the sale and moved on to the next sale. Nor did it devote time and attention to trying to develop a deeper understanding of the client's business and its problems and opportunities.

The property sales area has become to some degree commoditized. Few professionals in the business are likely to believe claims that a seller can always sell a property faster, at less cost and at higher prices than their competition. The individual acting for the client in this instance had come from a background in the insurance world, and was a quiet, studious individual. He placed great value on reliability and trust and had developed a solid professional relationship with the property services team. The Sales Behaviour Diagnosis profile of his expectations of a selling situation showed him placing relatively little value on product and a high value on relationships and partnership.

When the property sales team were presented with this data it was able to see the problem and, in a series of meetings to discuss the best way to approach the client, worked out an appropriate set of behaviours to employ. When the team was at last introduced to the client, his behaviour at the beginning of the meeting exhibited some degree of anxiety and uncertainty, but as the discussion progressed he began to relax, unfold his arms, and even to come out from behind his desk to join in a discussion about some points being put up on a whiteboard. Within six months he instructed the property sales team to sell two properties and help him acquire a third.

It depends upon the situation

Sales behaviours are situational. Sales success comes from matching sales behaviour to the behavioural expectations and preferences of the client. Think about what behaviours the customer would connect with. The good news is that you can measure this. You can also measure how your sales force behaves and whether there is a match or a mismatch between sales behaviours and customer preferences. Behaviour is observable, measurable and manageable. That is a key message of Behaviour Kinetics.

15

From recruitment profiling to talent management

Chris Dunn and Andy Pellant
AdviserPlus

AdviserPlus is a consultancy *that creates bespoke behavioural diagnostics for clients. It describes its approach as 'beyond psychometrics or personality profiling'. Its work focuses on identifying at the outset of a project the 'excellence' factors involved in success in any given role. It does this by identifying the critical behaviours, motivations, aspirations, skills and knowledge relevant to the role in question, which it then uses to model three key tools:*

- *a customized application form*
- *an excellence behavioural profile*
- *a recruitment and selection system.*

It transforms the profiles it builds into management tools for the client. Their focus is on work that is research based, trackable/measurable and robust. The profiles it creates are combined with the client's management database, providing the potential to capture data and to relate profile results to induction, training, development, learning and communication.

The approach of AdviserPlus is to create a process and profiling tool to help a client select, recruit and retain the most appropriate or 'best fit' people for a particular role. To do this it focuses on two things: role context and situation, and defining excellence. To understand role context and situation, it asks the following questions:

- What does this person have to do and how do they need to behave to deliver?
- In what environment and culture are they going to operate?
- How do you want them 'to be' as partners/franchisees/employees?

To define excellence it asks:

- Who best does the above and why?
- What do you know about them motivationally, behaviourally and functionally?
- What do you see?
- What do you feel?
- What do you want more or less of?

Dealer excellence at Snap-On Tools

In 2000 Snap-On Tools identified high dealer turnover (around 34 percent) as a key performance problem. The high dealer turnover was in turn related to unsatisfactory dealer van yield, which translated into lower returns, higher costs and diffusion of management time, energy and focus. Snap-On has approximately 400 dealers in the UK and each one turns over about £250k. As with any large group of individuals, performance ranged along a spectrum from unsatisfactory to good to excellent.

The contract between AdviserPlus and Snap-On Tools was to deliver an 'Index of dealer excellence'. In operational terms that translated into:

- identifying what dealer excellence looks like;
- converting this into a recruitment/selection system that could be run at branch level;
- training managers in the use of the profiling system.

The process was as follows. For the dealers, each potential dealer completed an application form and an online behavioural profile. This typically was done as part of the interview process. Different branches adopted slightly different approaches, some completing it prior to Interview 1 and others prior to Interview 2. It was completed at the branch in a supervised setting.

For the franchise managers, the steps involved were:

■ profile report on each applicant and special questions supplied for the interviews;

■ up-to-date information as required on potential;

■ access to enable review of all past profiles and to look at bio data;

■ a training programme for field managers, focusing on how to interview successfully and also how to use the profile information to manage dealer performance.

To identify what dealer excellence looked like, AdviserPlus profiled around 20 percent of the dealer population. To convert the findings into a recruitment/selection system that could be run at branch level (six branches), an application form and profiling tool were developed. And to train managers in the use of the profiling system an administration and management guide were produced.

The Snap-On curve

The profile of the 'ideal' dealer was originally researched and created in 2000. Research was based on qualitative and quantitative metrics between those dealers that performed well and those that did not. The curve that was established was used as the benchmark of 'recruitment excellence' for several years. The validity of the 'curve' was enhanced as more new dealers were recruited within this shape and went on to do well. Those that were recruited outside this recommended shape often failed and/or left the business. Additional research in 2004 allowed the profile to be refined.

The key roles of a Snap-On dealer are to *sell tools* and *collect money*. There are also the requirements of administration, small company accounting, customer service and team-working. Specifically, dealers need to:

- operate on their own – following pre-set and repetitive call patterns to establish reliability and to create demand;

- follow ways of working that are well established within the franchise system, which does not allow for innovation or creativity;

- operate largely alone with more and more of their management being done by technology-based telephony and PC-based solutions;

- be careful about who they do business with and how they manage outstanding debts.

The curve allows Snap-On to see how the dealer role/spec. is supported by the actual behaviour.

The Snap-On curve is shown in Figure 15.1.

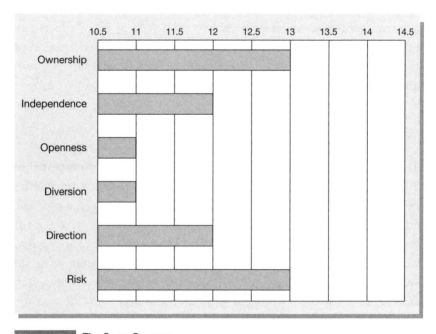

Figure 15.1 The Snap-On curve

Figure 15.1 shows the following:

■ High personal ownership – matched by an aversion to taking unnecessary risks.

■ Enough independence and direction to improve motivation and drive, but not too much that it creates unrest or a desire to 'do it differently'.

■ Enough openness to create good client relationships, but a strong sense of boundaries and structures that support the core message of repetitive call pattern, selling tools and collecting money.

■ Low levels of diversion that stop the dealer wanting to go off and do something else whenever they have a bad week.

Follow-up research

Over 2004–5 follow-up research was completed. It showed the following:

■ Dealer turnover had been cut by 50 percent (this equates to a saving of approximately £2,000,000 annually).

■ Yield per van (sales) 2002–3 were increased by 107 percent.

■ Yield per van (sales) 2003–4 were increased by 111 percent.

■ The company is now ranked as one of the top five in the British Franchise Association (BFA).

The research confirmed the following things about assessment ratings based on the behaviour profile of the curve:

■ There is a strong positive correlation between success, retention and positive assessment rating.

■ There is a strong positive correlation between poor performance, churn and negative assessment ratings.

■ There is a strong correlation between individuals who were recruited without being matched to the curve and poor performance and early termination.

As a result of the above, the following was agreed:

- To put the system online (it was originally done locally on a CD).

- To update and extend the profile.

- To extend the information fields so that branches can monitor and track recruitment and selection statistics, performance data and attrition data by field manager, thereby creating a 'dealer management system'.

16

The relationship between behaviour and managerial achievement

Professor Rick Roskin
University Canada West

Dr Rick Roskin is a Canadian academic, author and consultant who has studied and written about leadership behaviour and its relationship to achievement for more than 30 years. His book Managerial Achievement broke through the tight boundaries that academics and writers tend to place around motivation, communication and leadership and presented an integrated analysis of what managers do, centred on the match between their behaviour and the demands of their jobs and roles. He was an early proponent of Behaviour Kinetics principles, creating and developing change through the application of diagnostic tools that enable individuals and groups to identify their current behaviour and visualize what they need to do to improve their performance – or, to use his terminology, to improve managerial achievement.

At a seminar I once attended, the presenter said he had a friend who, instead of the typical telephone answering machine had a 'questioning machine'. If you phoned the friend, the machine's recorded message said, 'Hello, you've reached my questioning machine. I have two questions to ask: who are you, and what do you want?' Then, with an 'I gotcha' look on his face, the presenter went on to say that 95 percent of people could not answer these two questions.

In one sense these questions form the basis of Behaviour Kinetics because, as has been stated earlier in this book, 'You can't get there from here if you don't know where here is'. An accurate perception of the present creates potential for change and greatly increases the probability of actually ending up where you want to go. Otherwise success is purely based on fate and luck – especially the latter. The question 'What do you want?' is important because it raises the issue of developing a match between what the individual desires and what the organization needs. If finding the answer to these questions is dependent on divining an individual's great inner secrets through psychoanalysis or poring over personality profiles, then there is little hope for the process. However, as a number of examples in this book demonstrate, if you can create a simple but well-researched diagnostic questionnaire technology, getting the answers becomes relatively straightforward.

We all know that the best predictor of future behaviour is past behaviour and it is much easier to observe and measure behaviour than personality. But, as is always the case with complex human behaviour, our observations have to be as sophisticated as the people we are evaluating, because study after study has found that while personality is one of the many forces that drives behaviour, its influence is far less than popular belief would have it.

Pareto's Law – the '80/20 rule' – says that 20 percent of the energy, activity, and resources applied in a job or organization produce 80 percent of the results, while 80 percent of the activity and resources only manage to produce 20 percent of the outputs. The 80/20 rule applies to almost every job; 80 percent of what you do tends to produce 20 percent of your results. But that doesn't have to be the case. The answer is to focus on the critical areas of a job – where effort produces high pay-off – and apply your effort and resources there. So we define managerial achievement as: the degree to which a manager produces a high level of results in the critical areas of their job.

The Mach One system

The system we have developed to help mangers focus on the critical elements of their jobs, and thereby increase their level of achievement, is called Mach One. It has two main dimensions. It focuses on:

■ the manager's job and the important results that must be achieved within it;

■ the behaviour the manager exhibits in getting the job done.

Without a clear concept of the job and the knowledge of where effort needs to be applied to obtain high pay-offs (that is, a perception of the 'right' things to do in the job), and without a knowledge of how to behave in order to reach these goals, high achievement can never occur. Mach One is a Behaviour Kinetics application technology. It gets people to identify their observable, measurable behaviour and to identify the behaviour that is required to optimize achievement in their job. It is an 'ask them' technology. The individual is the data source and the ultimate job designer.

Style focus

The Mach One system is based on the research finding that there are three primary factors that underlie all managerial behaviour and all managerial jobs. All managerial behaviour is concerned to some degree with:

■ *Relationships with people* – an emphasis on encouraging, coaching, listening, cooperating, trusting and accepting relationships with others. We call this Red behaviour because it is emotional, empathic and warm. Like the red bulb in a traffic light, you have to stop and spend time developing these elements.

■ *Assessing the situation* – an emphasis on teams and on the processes and procedures of tasks and organization, on coordination and synthesis of the various elements in a work situation. We call this Amber behaviour because, like the amber bulb in a traffic light, it causes you to pause and think, to alter pace, to assess whether to stop or start.

■ *Getting the task accomplished* – an emphasis on telling people what to do, and what is expected of them, of directing, controlling and structuring their activities. We call this Green behaviour because it is all go, as reflected by the green bulb in a traffic light.

If you think about how you behave as a manager and about how others above, beside and below you in your organization behave, you will recognize instances of Red behaviour (listening to subordinates' problems, giving advice, operating an 'open door' style of management, getting employee input on important decisions through building consensus, encouraging, coaching and assisting); Amber behaviour (assessing situations and problems, coordinating, bringing conflicting parties and views together, using more of a consultation form of decision making, negotiating and planning); and Green behaviour (giving orders, telling people what to do and when to do it, implementing decisions quickly, checking on the activities of others, and making unilateral decisions without much consultation of any kind).

All managers exhibit these types of behaviours to some degree. Some are highly people-oriented and are reluctant to give direct orders or to initiate actions. Some spend almost all their time planning and coordinating the activities of those around them, and thinking and analyzing. And others are completely task-centred and show a very focused approach. The degree to which a person uses one or a combination of the basic approaches to managing is largely determined by a given circumstance and is not based on an either–or choice.

We use a triangle to display both an individual's behaviour (style) and the behavioural (style) demands of the job. The map is shaded from the apex (bulls-eye) towards the base, with an increasing number reflecting

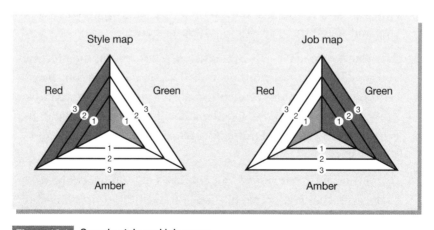

Figure 16.1 Sample style and job maps

a greater emphasis on the behaviour. In Figure 16.1, the style map (a map showing the balance of the individual's current behaviour) indicates an emphasis on Red behaviour (3 degrees), Green behaviour (1 degree), and Amber behaviour (zero degrees). The job map shows that the behaviour required to manage the job most effectively demands 3 degrees of Green behaviour, 2 degrees of Amber behaviour and 1 degree of Red behaviour. We have a major behaviour/job mismatch here.

Job focus

However, before you can decide the best style of behaviour to manage your job, you have to know what behaviour the job requires. You must have a clear and straightforward method of looking at your job and determining where you should focus your energies and attention. Mach One has developed an effective means of doing this. We have been able to identify 27 elements that can be used to describe any managerial job (see Table 16.1). They represent a comprehensive list of the basic processes which, when applied appropriately, lead to achievement. Each of these elements can be related to one of the underlying bases of management, so that some are Red processes, some Amber processes and some Green processes.

Table 16.1   Critical achievement elements

Red	Amber	Green
Advice	Change	Champion
Collaboration	Coordination	Control
Discussion	Delegation	Direction
Empowerment	Evaluation	Implementation
Encouragement	Forecasting	Objectives
Innovation	Negotiation	Performance
Listening	Planning	Persuasion
Mentoring	Quality	Production
Morale	Strategy	Quantity

Mach One says that a job can be analyzed in terms of the critical processes required for high achievement, and that each of these processes is the result of certain types of behaviour. Mach One therefore looks at achievement from two sides – the requirements of the job and the behaviour of the manager. They are linked by the fact that both can be described in terms of types of managerial behaviour: Red, Amber or Green.

The 27 critical achievement elements (CAEs) used in Mach One to analyze managerial jobs help answer the question 'What critical management processes will lead to high achievement in my job?' Once the CAE results are converted to required degrees of Red, Amber, and/or Green behaviour, the result is a job map.

Every manager has a particular set of objectives to meet. They define the job. If you want to know what an individual's job is, it is better to ask what it is that has to be achieved in the job rather than to ask what the job title is. To define a job, you have to know what it is supposed to produce and what its hoped-for results or objectives are. When we talk about the 'job' we mean: the organizational outputs over which a manager has formal authority and responsibility.

for high achievement to occur, you have to have a constant fix on your job

Jobs change over time. That is, the goals over which a manager has formal authority and responsibility change, and therefore the corresponding outputs, processes and activities change. For high achievement to occur, you have to have a constant fix on your job. Managers who do not have a clear picture of their jobs tend to manage them inappropriately; they may do things that are no longer necessary or may focus on unimportant aspects of the job.

Analyzing the job

Clearly, each job within an organization demands a particular type of managerial behaviour. Some aspects of a job are more important than others and could be considered critical to effective performance. The 27 critical achievement elements represent a checklist of potential avenues to high pay-offs that you, as a manager, should consider when you are assessing how to handle your job. Of course, you cannot and should not focus on all of them simultaneously. No job is that broad (at least no manageable job). But every job entails some of these elements, and failure to recognize which ones are relevant and which are less important can lead to stress and failure.

In every job some elements are absolutely essential to high achievement. Without them you simply cannot do a first-class job. They must be made the top-priority items in any analysis. There are other things that are important but are not absolutely essential. We tend to do lots of things that are not critical but because we like to do them. The goal is to gain focus and essentially to 'shrink the job' by doing the 'right' things.

Management style and achievement

Although it is useful to know the basis of a manager's style, we also want to be able to determine how effective the manager is in the application of that basic style. Achievement has two elements. The first and most important factor in achievement is the match between the behavioural demands of the job and the style and behaviour of the manager. For example, in Figure 16.1 the match between the manager's style map and job map is poor. The second aspect of achievement is the way in which the basic behaviour is displayed.

We all know managers who are very Green. Some of them achieve a great deal while others arouse nothing but hostility. Clearly there are different ways of showing Green behaviour. The same applies to Red behaviour. Sometimes a Red manager uses it to achieve positive results through the development of skilled and competent subordinates, and the stimulation of innovation, creativity and commitment, while on other occasions Red managers waste their energies trying hard to be liked by everyone and avoiding conflict at all costs. The former achieves a great deal, whereas the latter achieves little or nothing. The effective Amber manager focuses on getting processes, policies and systems working properly and on establishing groups and teams that interact well and achieve synergy. But Amber behaviour can also result in paralysis through analysis, and can become cold and be seen as distanced and unconcerned. Consequently, there are ranges of Red, Amber and Green behaviours that influence the level of achievement a manager can attain.

Style flexibility

Managers are more or less flexible in their response to the job and some can act effectively over a range of demands while others display consistent behaviour irrespective of the demand. The greater the range of behaviour over the three orientations, the greater the flexibility. However, effectiveness is dependent upon the appropriate match between the demands of the job and the style of behaviour displayed. The objective, therefore, is to have managers 'stretch their style' to give them the opportunity to maximize the result.

Empassionment and extreme achievement

We have all heard about empowerment – that to achieve a high level of commitment to the job, some degrees of freedom are necessary. In other words, some time must be available to allow the manager to take serious control of the job, and to escape the press of the routine. Mach One strives to get the manager one level beyond this to what we call 'empassionment'. This can only occur where shrinking the job and stretching the style allows the time to engage the innovative side of enterprise, which harnesses the deepest level of commitment possible and drives the greatest achievement. This is where the mind, body and soul all work in unison towards the same outcome. This is where the manager is almost into a 24/7/365 effort and does what must be done. This is the extreme achievement zone that only a few of us participate within, or find, for long. When we do get 'in the zone', we should analyze the elements that led to this zone to see if any of them can be harnessed for the future.

A case study

A large Canadian food processing company wanted to introduce team-based management to its packaging division. If successful, there were plans to migrate it to other divisions as well.

The project was initiated by a steering committee, with representation from management, the union, employees and customers. It was decided that senior management should be the first to engage the process so as to reflect commitment, and so that local union representation would be encouraged to become involved. To satisfy the union and its representatives, and to make everyone more comfortable, the Mach One consultants met with all those who wished, either individually or in groups, to take part in the process. Following Behaviour Kinetics principles, each individual was asked to identify critical issues facing them and the company. These were then all addressed by integrating them into the design of the interventions – meetings, presentations and workshops. On the basis of this, all resistance to participation dropped away and the local union stewards decided to engage in the process and take part in all activities.

The opening stage of the process involved managers, staff and union representatives completing a set of Mach One behavioural diagnostics. This enabled each individual to identify their current style of behaviour and, most importantly, to identify the behaviour they felt would be most appropriate to manage their jobs effectively. This data was then fed back to individuals in small groups. A job map was developed for each individual (on the basis of what *they* had identified as the critical elements of their jobs) and they were then able to match that with their style map and discuss the compatibility or incompatibility and what to do about it.

This process always makes the move from 'So what?' to 'What now?. It leads to a focus on what actions each individual needs to take to 'do a better job' and results in action plans to which each person feels highly committed, not simply because the actions will lead to improved effectiveness on the job but also because they give people control over their lives, their work and their destiny. It is highly energizing.

Team building versus team-based leadership

The next stage in the process was focused on evaluating teams and developing strategies to help them improve their performance. Building on a base of individual understanding of team members' behaviour, and assessing the behavioural balance required to achieve a high level of team performance, teams were able to agree and commit to a variety of actions designed to help them work more effectively and maintain a higher level of goal achievement.

I have always believed that to advertise an intervention as 'team building' seems, and is, superficial. The idea that 'On Monday, after our team building event, we will all be a team' is social engineering gone mad. By generating and practising the type of behaviour that leads to success, and by creating a sense of achievement and commitment, working groups build themselves into teams. This is especially true when the reward system parallels the desired outcomes.

> **" by creating a sense of achievement and commitment, working groups build themselves into teams "**

In the case of the food processing company, teams developed codes of conduct. These codes focused on how to treat each other, how to do the right things, and how to do things right. When matters went awry, the teams evaluated their behaviour and performance in relation to their code of conduct. This process helped teams address what they termed 'the execution of the promise'.

Minor technological innovation

Few interventions I have been involved with create a circumstance where the outcome allows a clear measure of effect. There seem to be too many variables to allow a clean determination, although anecdotal and limited calculations can be made. However, this was a unique situation because million-dollar packaging machines had been purchased and had been in operation for several months. The machines had achieved the manufacturer's specification of 120,000 pounds of product per week, although it took some time to reach that level and initially it had been difficult to get beyond 90,000 pounds.

Following the Mach One process, plant managers noticed the numbers climbing. It became clear that there was a friendly competition occurring between plants. Eventually one plant was able to raise machine output to 190,000 pounds and the average of all plants stabilized at 175,000 pounds. This productivity so amazed the US manufacturer that it sent its technical people to find out what was happening. It turned out that a number of minor technological innovations had been introduced by the teams and these had allowed the increase in productivity. This is a clear example of the result of an 'ask them' style of management. It demonstrates how attention to the principles of Behaviour Kinetics leads to results and to management and staff all emerging as winners.

References

J. Stewart Black and Hal B. Gregerson, *Leading Strategic Change: Breaking Through the Brain Barrier* (Financial Times Prentice Hall, 2002).

A. Caspi, O. Harrington, B. Milne, J. Amell, R. Theodore and T. Moffit, 'Children's behavioural styles at age three are linked to their adult personality traits at age 26', *Journal of Personality*, Volume 71, Issue 4 (August 2003).

Dan Ciampa, 'Almost ready: how leaders move up', *Harvard Business Review* (January 2005).

Jim Collins, *Good to Great* (Random House, 2001).

Stephen P. Covey, *The Seven Habits of Highly Effective People* (Simon & Schuster, 1989).

Stanley M. Davis and Paul R. Lawrence, *Matrix* (Addison-Wesley, 1977).

Peter Drucker, *Managing in Turbulent Times* (Harper & Row, 1980).

Daniel Druckman and Robert Bjork, *In the Mind's Eye: Enhancing Human Performance* (National Academy Press, 1991).

Bertram Forer, 'The fallacy of personal validation: a classroom demonstration of gullibility', *Journal of Abnormal Psychology*, 44 (1949), 118–121.

Doug Garr, *IBM Redux: Lou Gerstner and the Business Turnaround of the Decade* (HarperBusiness, 2000).

Harold Geneen with Alvin Moscow, *Management* (Granada Publishing, 1985).

Louis Gerstner, *Who Says Elephants Can't Dance? How I Turned Around IBM* (HarperCollins, 2003).

GoJobsite, 'Research highlights UK job insecurity', 20 May 2003.

F. Herzberg, B. Mausner and B. Snyderman, *The Motivation to Work* (Wiley, 1959).

Jon R. Katzenbach and Douglas K. Smith, *The Wisdom of Teams* (Harvard Business School Press, 1993).

John Kotter, *Leading Change* (Harvard Business School Press, 1996).

John Kotter, *The Heart of Change* (Harvard Business School Press, 2002).

Jeffrey K. Liker, *The Toyota Way* (McGraw-Hill, 2004).

Michael Mankins and Richard Steele, 'Turning great strategy into great performance', *Harvard Business Review* (July 2005).

Walter Mischel, *Personality and Assessment* (Lawrence Erlbaum, 1968).

Annie Murphy Paul, *The Cult of Personality* (Free Press, 2004).

Laurence Peter and Raymond Hull, *The Peter Principle* (Souvenir Press, 1994).

Rick Roskin, *Managerial Perception, Behaviour and Achievement: A Situational Orientation* (University of Bradford, 1977).

Rick Roskin, *Managerial Achievement* (Reston, 1983).

K.D. Ryan and D.K. Oestreich, *Driving Fear out of the Workplace* (Jossey-Bass, 1991).

James Surowiecki, *The Wisdom of Crowds* (Doubleday, 2004).

Index